AMERICA THROUGH FOREIGN EYES

AMERICA THROUGH FOREIGN EYES

CLASSIC INTERPRETATIONS OF AMERICAN POLITICAL LIFE

STEPHEN BROOKS

OXFORD
UNIVERSITY PRESS

OXFORD
UNIVERSITY PRESS

70 Wynford Drive, Don Mills, Ontario M3C 1J9
www.oup.com/ca

Oxford University Press is a department of the University of Oxford.
It furthers the University's objective of excellence in research, scholarship,
and education by publishing worldwide in

Oxford New York

Auckland Bangkok Buenos Aires Cape Town Chennai
Dar es Salaam Delhi Hong Kong Istanbul Karachi Kolkata
Kuala Lumpur Madrid Melbourne Mexico City Mumbai Nairobi
São Paulo Shanghai Singapore Taipei Tokyo Toronto

with an associated company in Berlin

Oxford is a trade mark of Oxford University Press in the UK and in certain other countries

Published in Canada by Oxford University Press

Copyright © Oxford University Press Canada 2002

The moral rights of the author have been asserted

Database right Oxford University Press (maker)

First published 2002

National Library of Canada Cataloguing in Publication Data

Brooks, Stephen, 1956–
    America through foreign eyes : classic interpretations of American political life

Includes bibliographical references and index.
ISBN 0-19-541229-X

1. United States—Civilization. 2. United States—Politics and government. 3. United
States—Foreign public opinion. I. Title

E169.1.B8 2002   973   C2001-903183-1

Cover & Text Design: Brett J. Miller
1 2 3 4 – 05 04 03 02
This book is printed on permanent (acid-free) paper ∞.
Printed in Canada

CONTENTS

To my students
in American politics

PREFACE

As a teacher I have often been frustrated that my students have not read—indeed, usually have not been given the opportunity to read—the classic interpretations of American politics. They have heard of Alexis de Tocqueville, but few have read his masterly *Democracy in America*. They probably know, at least by their senior year, the names of such great interpreters of the American political tradition as Frederick Jackson Turner and Charles Beard, but unless they have taken a specialized course on the historical development of American political culture or the history of the United States Constitution, they are unlikely to have more than a vague idea of the contribution of these figures to understanding the American political tradition. Their education too often skips over or lightly touches upon some of the greatest interpreters of American politics.

This, everyone who teaches American politics and history agrees, is a shame. There is no replacement for reading the original writings of great thinkers. But in an age of textbook learning and highly specialized courses and programs, the opportunity to do so seldom exists for most students.

This book is a modest attempt to expose students to some of the great interpretations of American politics, by foreigners whose works are widely acknowledged in the United States and abroad to be among the most perceptive analyses ever written. The inclusion of Alexis de Tocqueville, Lord James Bryce, Harold Laski, and Gunnar Myrdal—a Frenchman, two Englishmen, and a Swede—requires no justification. Their work continues to be routinely cited by historians, political scientists, sociologists, and others who study the politics and society of the United States. Simone de Beauvoir's name is less often linked to America, but the fascinating interpretation that she wrote of her first visit to the United States is, I believe, worthy of inclusion in this elite company. Of course, the list of foreigners who have written about the United States is almost endless, and includes such prominent thinkers as Karl Marx, Werner Sombart, André Siegfried, G.K. Chesterton, H.G. Wells, Jacques Maritain . . . the list goes on and on. In restricting myself to five among many, I have been guided by a few considerations. First, I wished to select writers who are without question among the most widely cited foreign interpreters of American politics and history, and whose analyses have withstood the test of time as measured by the questions, 'Can we still learn from them today? Does the picture they paint provide us with flashes of recognition and insight into the contemporary scene in America?' Second, I chose writers whose observations about America chiefly reveal something about its politics, as opposed to its culture or institutions examined in ways that do not attempt to link these to political life. Third, I have tried to write a book that can be used in a range of courses on American politics, history, and society. The questions of how and why astute foreign observers have interpreted American politics and society in the ways they have are important across disciplines, and as likely to be asked in a first-year introduction to American Politics as in a senior-level course on American political culture.

The book begins with a chapter entitled 'America Through Foreign Eyes', in which I attempt to explain what is now a centuries-old fascination that America has held for foreigners. Some of the historical meanings that have been associated with America are examined, followed by an explanation of the unique contribution that the foreigner's perspective can bring to an understanding of America.

The five subsequent chapters are devoted to the writings of Tocqueville, Bryce, Myrdal, Laski, and Beauvoir, respectively. In introducing readers to their ideas I explain who they were, what motivated them to write about America, the historical and intellectual context within which their observations were made, and, finally and most importantly, the main lines of their respective interpretations of American politics and society. In every case I aim to show how their writings are important not merely as historical snapshots of America, but because they continue to provide insight into the America of today.

My plan is that this book will be the first part in a two-part series on *America Through Foreign Eyes*. The second volume will be devoted to more recent foreign interpretations of the American scene, including French, British, Russian, Canadian, and Chinese perspectives on the United States. As this was first drafted (November 2000) the eyes of the world's press were glued to the American presidential election, the outcome of which was being decided in a three-ring circus of lawyers, Florida courts, and the court of American public opinion, all mediated by CNN and an army of talking heads and television images. No one who seeks to write today about the state of the world and the trajectory of history can ignore the United States, and none seek to do so.

This book has been a number of years in the making while I thought and rethought what I wanted to achieve and how best to accomplish it. The project finally came together during a sabbatical spent at the University of Michigan, Ann Arbor. To the Department of Political Science at the University of Michigan, I wish to express my thanks for the hospitality extended to me. To my students in Political Science 496, 'Foreign Perspectives on American Politics', my thanks for your patience while I tried out my ideas on you and for your observations and reactions. You helped to sharpen my thinking about American politics and I trust that you, too, learned something along the way.

The people I have worked with at Oxford University Press have been patient beyond what could reasonably have been expected. In particular I wish to thank Euan White, Phyllis Wilson, and Laura Macleod, all of whom have had a hand in encouraging me to finish this book. Richard Tallman has been my copy editor for several books, spanning more than a decade. His sharp eye and thoughtful suggestions are greatly appreciated.

I also wish to thank the three reviewers for this book. Their comments were among the most helpful that I have ever received on a manuscript. Along with my students at Michigan and various colleagues with whom I have discussed this book, they are, of course, blameless for its inadequacies.

Barbara Faria and Lorraine Cantin, both of the University of Windsor, keyboarded the manuscript and its revisions. As I have acknowledged in other books, their efficiency and good humor, when the pressures of work could have excused something much less, has been unfailing. I am grateful to them.

My greatest debt is owed to the Fulbright Foundation. Being chosen a Visiting Fulbright Scholar in 2000 provided me with the circumstances I needed to complete this project. I hope the fruit of my labor during that period will repay in some modest way the Foundation's generosity.

Stephen Brooks
Ann Arbor and Sorrento's (Windsor)

Chapter 1

ॐ

THE MEANING OF AMERICA

The world is fascinated by America. Its culture and values are exported throughout the world, through film and popular music, in advertising and fashion, and by the corporate symbolism of trademarks and logos. No other society has, or has had, the remarkable reach of the United States when it comes to cultural influence. And no other society has, or has had, such a powerful impact on the imaginations of people throughout the world. As Ignacio Ramonet writes:

> How could it fail to fascinate us? The United States has powerful resources with which to excite our envy and enchant our hearts and minds. In political terms, it has the amiable countenance of an old and accommodating democracy, heir to a revolution of universal significance and a rich culture. For millions of oppressed people all over the world, its famous symbol—Liberty lighting the world—still represents a powerful message of hope and the promise of a better life.[1]

The world's fascination with America does not stop at consuming the products, images, and stories that it exports to markets beyond its borders. More books have been written by foreigners about America, as have more foreign newspaper and magazine articles, and more television and radio news stories and documentaries have been produced about all aspects of American society, than can be said of any other society. During the writing of this book the 2000 election took place in the United States. Interested to know what the rest of the world thought about the campaign and the contenders for the American presidency, I regularly trolled the mass media in several countries, including Canada, the United Kingdom, France, and Belgium. In the major newspapers of all of these countries there was extensive coverage of the American election campaign, in some cases reaching well back into 1999 when the pre-primaries jockeying between candidates had already begun. Newspapers such as *The Guardian*,

The Economist, and *The Times* in England, *Le Monde* in France, the *Globe and Mail* and the *National Post* in Canada, and *Le Soir* in Belgium devoted dozens of articles to the American elections. The evening of the election the Canadian Broadcasting Corporation and France 2 were among the television networks that carried live coverage of the returns. This is, of course, an extreme form of flattery: to acknowledge that another country's politics and elections matter so much and, presumably, will interest enough viewers to broadcast foreign election results live.

Americans, it must be said, are not in the habit of repaying the compliment. They are not particularly fascinated by or knowledgeable about the rest of the world. An American professor once said to me that his students, whose methodological skills and sophistication were sharp, tended to view other countries as so much real estate. This is an approach to the rest of the world that can only exist in a society whose cultural self-sufficiency is great. Foreigners are inclined to characterize American ignorance or indifference toward the rest of the world as arrogant and parochial. But if Americans tend to think of the rest of the world in terms of trade opportunities, security threats, and vacation destinations, without the world outside the United States leaving much of an impression on their own sense of who they are, this is not very surprising. The United States is the great power of our era, the only country whose cultural, political, economic, and military influence extends across the globe. Moreover, America has a historical meaning in the eyes of the world that is unmatched by another society. The Soviet Union provided an alternative pole in the imagination of the contemporary world, but its collapse left the United States unrivaled as what Ignacio Ramonet calls 'the only remaining hyperpower'.[2]

Those of us who do not live in the United States may be forgiven if we occasionally appear sensitive about Americans' ignorance and incuriosity in regard to our own societies. Impressions gathered from surveys of students taking American Politics at universities in Canada and Belgium confirmed this sensitivity.[3] Asked the question, 'What if any features of American politics, culture, or society do you dislike?', some of the comments included the following:

- The way US imperialism wants to control the world.
- Apathy toward world affairs.
- They seem to be too egocentric.... The President is referred to as the leader of the free world, which is sometimes offensive to other nationalities.

- Americans seem to feel that they are the rulers of the world and all of our saviors.
- Arrogance/thinking they are superior.
- They have no conception of the outside world and their place in it.
- American cheerleading (too much patriotism).
- American arrogance in international relations.
- I find it shocking that Americans are often unable to describe what's going on in the rest of the world.

At the same time there was much that these non-American students admired about the United States. Among the features of American politics, culture, and society that received favourable mention were the following:

- the high standard of living
- friendliness of the people
- patriotism
- emphasis on rights and freedoms
- diversity of American society
- competitiveness, creativity, and entrepreneurialism
- the fact that they haven't invaded us in over 185 years! [from a Canadian]

Clearly, foreigners often have ambivalent feelings about America. The United States has the ability to excite in outsiders contradictory feelings of admiration and repugnance. Leonard Cohen's characterization of America as 'the cradle of the best and of the worst' captures this ambivalence, an ambivalence I personally have encountered on countless occasions among my students in Canada and Belgium. These impressions and judgments of America are nothing new. One finds this ambivalence in the writings of many of the early European visitors to America, including the writings of Alexis de Tocqueville. It is the fascination occasioned by that which is irresistible, but at the same time repulsive or threatening in some way.

As the devastating attack of September 11, 2001, showed, when hijacked commercial airliners hit the twin towers of New York's World Trade Center, reducing them to rubble, and another jet plane was piloted by terrorists into the Pentagon, America is an object of hatred among some foreigners and in some corners of the world. This is a relatively recent phenomenon. The United States government and its foreign policies have often, and for many years, generated anger and hatred abroad, going back at least to the war with Mexico in the mid-nineteenth century. Moreover, the propaganda machines of the early Soviet Union under Lenin and Stalin and in Nazi Germany portrayed the United States as an enemy and threat to the interests and values of the Soviet and German people, respectively. But hatred of *Americans*—of their values and way of life—is more recent. It has been only since World War II and the emergence of the United States as the unquestioned leader of the capitalist West that the American people and their culture, and not merely the policies of their governments, have become targets for hatred in some foreign circles.

As the global reach of America's power has widened, culturally, economically, politically, and militarily, this has produced a reaction among some who believe that the values and institutions that comprise America threaten them in some way. The perceived threat may be to foreigners' economic interests, political independence, or cultural integrity. From European left-wing intellectuals, who generally heap scorn on America, to Osama bin Laden and those who have openly called for the murder of Americans and the destruction of the pillars of American-led Western civilization, this reaction to the global influence of America has gained strength over the last half-century. For their part, most Americans have been blissfully ignorant of, and perhaps even indifferent toward, the world's opinion of them. In some ways this is odd. Tocqueville and other earlier visitors to America frequently commented on how Americans were eager to know what others thought of them and their country, and were often sensitive and defensive in the face of criticisms. It may be that one of the consequences of becoming the world's only remaining superpower has been to desensitize Americans to the world's opinion. In any event, the tragedy of September 11, 2001, brought home to all Americans the sobering truth: they are not universally loved, nor can they afford to ignore the hatred that is felt toward them in some corners of the world.

AMERICA IN THE WORLD

America has occupied a place near the center of the modern imagination of the Western world for several centuries. This began during the Age of Exploration, when Christopher Columbus, Amerigo Vespucci, John Cabot, and others touched the shores of what would come to be thought of as the New World. America early on acquired a meaning—or meanings—in the eyes of the world, which constituted an important part of the mindscape of the West. The original meaning attributed to America, as the eastern edge of the Orient, a world known to the West from the time of Marco Polo and the spice trading routes that snaked across Asia, turned out to be mistaken. But this meaning was soon replaced by others.

The realization that the Atlantic coast of America was not the Orient caused some disappointment. Hopes that gold and diamonds might be found in this part of the New World proved to be equally groundless. Instead, there were fish, animal furs, and timber, all of which would become important exports from America to Europe, but none of which generated either the excitement or zeal for conquest and expansion that the gold and other riches of the Aztec and Inca empires inspired in the Spanish.

The lack of gold, diamonds, and civilizations whose accumulated wealth would have attracted the interest of conquistadors and seekers after bullion proved fortunate for the future course of what would become the United States. Those who established the first important European settlements at Virginia and Massachusetts Bay were drawn by both the hope of material gain and freedom. The desire for material gain was the factor that led people to emigrate from England to Virginia, which soon developed a plantation economy that used slaves imported from West Africa—thus sowing the seeds of America's greatest and most intractable political dilemma. The Plymouth Plantation on Massachusetts Bay was settled by English religious dissidents who left their exile in Leyden (Netherlands) for the New World in order more freely to practice their religion. Thus it was that the beginnings of the United States were marked by two impulses that have characterized America ever since, and that virtually all European observers have remarked upon—freedom and material gain. They are aspirations that would quickly become synonymous with America.

To the Europeans who arrived in the colony of Virginia, America meant the prospect of gain. Some were nothing more than adventurers motivated by the hope of a quick fortune—a very American hope that lives on today in the dreams of Internet day traders, Silicon Valley entrepreneurs, and other heirs to one of America's oldest dreams. To the Pilgrim Fathers who established the Plymouth Plantation, America meant the freedom to build a social order according to their moral precepts. They saw themselves as a chosen people under the providence of God, another meaning of America that has persisted over the centuries. For the West African slaves imported into Virginia and other colonies, the meaning of America had nothing to do with material gain, freedom, or a

providential mission. America meant forced separation from their original home and oppression by white Europeans. This, too, is a meaning of
America that has endured over time, despite the abolition of slavery, an
end to legal segregation on racial lines, and the undeniable improvement
in the education, living standards, and participation of African
Americans in American society. Racial inequality continues to be one of
the meanings of America.

Many nations and countries can boast of great military, economic, or
cultural accomplishments. Some nations established and maintained
empires that spanned enormous distances and several centuries. Even
today the capitals of these empires—Rome, Athens, Constantinople,
Alexandria, London, and others—evoke memories of past greatness.
Some see the United States as being merely the latest great imperial power:
a sort of 'globo-cop' in military affairs; an economic powerhouse without
equal for more than a century; and the home base of a homogenizing cultural juggernaut that lays waste to local traditions and lifestyles and
replaces them with McDonald's, Disney, and Microsoft.

The meaning of America and the unique contribution of the United
States to world history cannot be reduced, however, to superior missiles,
economic prowess, and an invasive mass culture. It rests instead on the
expectations that others have had, and continue to have, for America, and
on the expectations that Americans have held, and continue to hold, for
themselves. Expectations of greatness have been held for America from
the time when America was little more than an idea in the minds of
Europeans.

GREAT EXPECTATIONS

What does it mean to say that a country, people, society, or empire is
'great'? In an age of devalued words, when the latest pop musician's work
is described as 'great' or some accomplishment receives carpet-bombing
television coverage only to be eclipsed a week later by yet another 'great'
achievement, we need to establish what constitutes greatness.

By 'great' I mean the stuff of heroism, myth, and legend, all of which
are based on the striving for something beyond the normal bounds of the
human condition and the achievement of some form of immortality. The
quality of greatness lies in both the achievement and the aspiration, the
deed and the idea behind it. What makes the United States a great democracy and society are not merely its accomplishments, which are consider-

able, but the ideas and aspirations that America has embodied and continues to represent.

Greatness does not necessarily mean goodness. Julius Caesar was a great man, as Marc Anthony reminds the Roman mob in the funeral oration in Shakespeare's *Julius Caesar*, but as every reader of the play well knows, he also succumbed to the vice of ambition and was a tragic and ambiguous figure. Good and evil, virtue and vice, soaring success and abysmal failure may be combined in the character and history of one who achieves greatness.

The same is true of societies. No one can deny that America's long history of slavery and the legally sanctioned discrimination against African Americans, which lasted for much of the twentieth century, represents a major failure—the major failure—of American democracy. But it is because of the greatness of the principles on which American democracy was based, the equality of persons and the importance of individual freedom, that race relations are considered to be such a tragic failure of American society.

Swedish sociologist Gunnar Myrdal understood this when he wrote *An American Dilemma*. The tragedy and injustice of slavery and race discrimination in the United States were magnified by the fact that America's treatment of African Americans was so glaringly at odds with what Myrdal called the 'American creed', the principles of equality and freedom enshrined in the Declaration of Independence and invoked so regularly in American public life that they constituted a national ethos. The scale of the ambition encapsulated in Thomas Jefferson's declaration—'that all men are created equal, that they are endowed by their Creator with certain unalienable Rights, that among these are Life, Liberty, and the pursuit of Happiness'—was the standard of greatness against which racial discrimination would be measured. The greatness of the ideal stood in sharp contrast to a reality that seemed the antithesis of Jefferson's noble vision.

Great expectations have been held for America from the arrival of the Pilgrims of Massachusetts Bay. It goes without saying that these expectations have not been fully met and that, indeed, there have been major disappointments and disillusionments over the course of American history. Critics at home and abroad have been quick to pounce on such failures as slavery, class and racial inequality, and the Vietnam War to demonstrate what they argue is the hypocrisy or, at least, the unfulfilled nature of the ideals America is said to stand for.

But as Christopher Ricks and William Vance observe, 'Great disappointment has to be proportionate to greatness. What America promised, and fulfilled for many people, is implied in what is criticized: its failure to be all it promised.'[4] When critics sneer at the high rate of gun-related homicide in the United States, its enormous and disproportionately African-American prison population, its urban blight in places like Detroit, Newark, and south Chicago, and its health-care system that leaves about 40 million citizens without health insurance, they are implicitly measuring what they see as the failures of America against great ideals and high expectations.

Its failures, like its successes, are part of any fair-minded assessment of the American experience. But the meaning of America and its role in world history cannot be reduced to a balance sheet of accomplishments. The ideals associated with America are vital if we are to understand what makes it great.

THE MYTHIC CHARACTER OF AMERICA

'In the beginning all of the world was America.' This is how the English philosopher John Locke expressed the meaning of America. It was, Locke perceived, something as close to the mythical 'state of nature' that he, Jean-Jacques Rousseau, and other liberal thinkers wrote about as one was likely to find in the real world. America represented, for Locke, a sort of mythical counterpoint to the rigid stratification, decadence, and misery that characterized the lives of most people in the Old World. It was a tabula rasa, a clean slate, on which mankind would write a new chapter, whose story would be very different from all that previous civilizations had written. Here was the opportunity for men and women to reinvent themselves and their institutions, free from the dead hand of tradition, the shackles of class and social hierarchy, and the weight of centuries-old prejudices.

This is one of the original meanings of America that partakes of the quality of myth. America as the state of nature, the new opportunity and fresh start—for individuals and mankind—the escape from the past, the providential promised land: these were the ideas and aspirations that lifted to the higher plane of myth the prosaic reality of carving farms and roads out of an often inhospitable land. The accompanying box provides a sampling of some of these mythic characterizations from the pens of Europeans and Americans alike.

AMERICA AS A NEW CHAPTER IN THE HISTORY OF MANKIND

We hold these truths to be self-evident, that all men are created equal, that they are endowed by their Creator with certain unalienable Rights, that among these are Life, Liberty and the pursuit of Happiness.—That to secure these rights, Governments are instituted among Men, deriving their just powers from the consent of the governed,—That whenever any Form of Government becomes destructive of these ends, it is the Right of the People to alter or to abolish it, and to institute new Government, laying its foundation on such principles and organizing its powers in such form, as to them shall seem most likely to effect their Safety and Happiness.

—*DECLARATION OF INDEPENDENCE*, 1776

The revolution of America presented in politics what was only theory in mechanics. So deeply rooted were all the governments of the old world, and so effectively had the tyranny and the antiquity of habit established itself over the mind, that no beginning could be made in Asia, Africa, or Europe, to reform the political condition of man. Freedom had been hunted round the globe; reason was considered as rebellion; and the slavery of fear had made men afraid to think.

—THOMAS PAINE, *THE RIGHTS OF MAN*, 1792

America, you are luckier
Than this old continent of ours;
You have no ruined castles
And no volcanic earth.
You do not suffer
In hours of intensity
From futile memories
And pointless battles.
Concentrate on the present joyfully!
And when your children write books
May a good destiny keep them
From knight, robber, and ghost-stories.

—JOHANN WOLFGANG VON GOETHE, 'THE UNITED STATES', 1827

In America the great experiment of the attempt to construct society upon a new basis was to be made by civilized man; and it was there, for the first time, that theories hitherto unknown, or deemed impracticable, were to exhibit a spectacle for which the world had not been prepared by the history of the past.

—ALEXIS DE TOCQUEVILLE, *DEMOCRACY IN AMERICA*, VOL. 1, 1835

The mythic character of America is abundantly expressed in its own literature and that of other societies. Traditionally, America has represented freedom, the new beginning, escape, the possibility to become something or someone new and better, innocence, and purity. Some of these themes resonate less powerfully today, particularly innocence and purity, but this was bound to happen as America acquired historical baggage, not all of it welcome, that had not burdened it during its early years.

Indeed, the cynical and ironic temper of our times makes it difficult to accept at face value the expectations and ideals that were held for America during its youth. But as Fred Somkin demonstrates in *Unquiet Eagle*, such grand visions of America as a new form of civilization destined to influence all mankind were commonplace in the nineteenth century.[5] The New World had created a New Man free of the fetters of the past and with an unlimited future before him. The poet Grenville Mellen summed up the mood when he wrote,

> Still, tell me not of years of old,
> Of ancient hearth and clime;
> Ours is the land and age of gold,
> And ours the hallow'd time![6]

The mission of America was believed to be both political and spiritual. Politically, America's destiny was to build a republic of free men under a constitution creating the greatest democracy in the history of the world. Spiritually, the mission of America was to nurture what Thomas Jefferson called the New Man, whose soul was pure of the artifice and social distinctions characteristic of the Old World, and whose opportunities would be limited only by his desires and abilities.

A boundless optimism and confidence in the greatness and righteousness of America are commonplace in early American writings. Asked to describe the boundaries of his nation to a foreigner, the story goes that a Kentuckian once replied, 'Why sir, on the north we are bounded by the Aurora Borealis, on the east we are bounded by the rising sun, on the south we are bounded by the procession of the Equinoxes, and on the west by the Day of Judgement.'[7] The reference to 'the Day of Judgement' is particularly significant. American optimism and faith in the greatness of its society and institutions have long rested on the bedrock of Providence. America as a chosen land and Americans as a chosen people are elements of the mythic meaning of America. Even today, no American President would dare express the least doubt that the hand of divine Providence has steered the destiny of his country.

What I am calling the mythic character of America was perhaps best expressed by J. Hector St John de Crèvecoeur, a Frenchman who farmed for a couple of decades in New York state before returning to France in 1780. In his well-known *Letters from an American Farmer,* Crèvecoeur wrote:

> Here individuals of all nations are melted into a new race of men, whose labours and posterity will one day cause great change in the world. . . . The American is a new man, who acts upon new principles; he must therefore entertain new ideas, and form new opinions. From involuntary idleness, servile dependence, penury, and useless labour [in the Old World], he has passed to toils of a very different nature, rewarded by ample subsistence. This is an American.[8]

America as the 'melting pot', the crucible in which would emerge what Harvard historian Louis Hartz calls 'The First Universal Nation'—universal in that its national identity would be defined by its principles rather than by ethnicity, language, religion, or any of the other usual badges of nationality—this was one of the meanings of America that Crèvecoeur perceived during the infancy of the American republic. It is captured in the slogan on the seal of the President of the United States, 'E Pluribus Unum'—from the many, one. For most of America's history the idea of the melting pot has been viewed favorably, although critics and dissenters have been more numerous at various times, as during the middle to late nineteenth century, when the predominantly Northern European ethnic mix in the United States faced the challenge of absorbing increasing numbers of Southern and Eastern Europeans. In recent decades what the founders of the republic assumed to be one of America's virtues and unique contributions to the world has come under increasing pressure for reasons that have to do with changing patterns of immigration and changing ideology. Multiculturalism, a word virtually absent from the lexicon of American politics before the 1970s, today challenges the older vision of a universal nation. Nevertheless, America remains strong in its ability to integrate newcomers and reinvent itself in ways that are recognizably American, at the same time as the cultural baggage of immigrants alters the nature of American life.

UNDERSTANDING AMERICA

> No American can achieve detachment in studying America, and I doubt whether even a European or Asian can. Paraphrasing Lord Acton, one might say that the only detached student of American civilization would be a dead one, since he would no longer care. The best you can do to achieve perspective is to keep a certain emotional distance from your subject. When the subject is your own people and civilization it is hard to keep the distance. Your hopes and fears for America manage to break through and color the analysis.[9]

This book is written in the belief that some insights and perspectives on a society and its politics are best achieved—perhaps only achieved—through the eyes of outsiders. Like Max Lerner, from whom the above quotation is taken, I would not suggest that, when it comes to America at least, foreigners are more likely to be detached and free of emotional and ideological predispositions than Americans. Everyone brings something to the table so that a sort of Olympian detachment is probably, as Lerner suggests, impossible.

Nonetheless, the perspective that an astute and observant outsider can provide may be extremely valuable. There is no shortage of foreign observers of the American political scene, among them some of the most prominent historians, philosophers, and social scientists of the past two centuries. From at least the time of the American Revolution it became apparent that the trajectory of what Max Lerner called the *American civilization* would have important implications for the world and the history of mankind. Commentators have been divided on the nature of these implications, but no one denies that they have been enormous and perhaps even without parallel.

The five outside observers whose interpretations and writings are included in this book are all among the most often cited interpreters of American politics and society. They include Alexis de Tocqueville, Lord James Bryce, Gunnar Myrdal, Harold Laski, and Simone de Beauvoir. The amount of time that each spent in America varied from less than a year in the case of Tocqueville and Beauvoir to a couple of decades in the case of Laski. Their reasons for taking America as their subject varied and the particular aspects of American politics and society they focused on were different. But each left to succeeding generations, down to our own, a monumental analysis of America that has withstood the test of time. Modern readers cannot help but experience flashes of recognition when they read many of the passages from the writings of these significant foreign interpreters of the American political landscape. Indeed, this is part of what makes these five writers so important: their ability to penetrate to the essential and enduring nature of their subject.

Each of these writers contributes to our understanding of America, whether we are Americans or not. But Max Lerner's point about one's 'hopes and fears for America' operating as a filter that inevitably affects one's perceptions is as true for foreign observers as it is for their American counterparts. I am reminded of a remark by a Cuban-American filmmaker who made a documentary about the problem of identity confusion in his own family, divided between Cuba and Florida. 'If somebody were to paint a picture of you,' he said, 'you may or may not think that it looks like you. But I think that if you stare at it for hours, seeing the way somebody else sees you, then there is no way that you cannot learn something from that, whether you think that it looks like you or not.'[10] To which one might add that what you learn may not be only about you, the subject of the picture, but about the one who drew the picture and the nature of the emotional, psychological, and intellectual relationship between the subject and the observer. The following chapters are intended to help readers understand America, an America viewed through foreign eyes, but also to understand better why the world outside the United States has interpreted the American experience in the ways it has.

Alexis de Tocqueville came to America to study its prison system. He left to the world what would become the best-known and most often cited study of American politics ever written by a foreign visitor. (By Theodore Chasseriau (1819–56). Alexis de Tocqueville (1805–59), Historian. Photo: Arnaudet. Châteaux de Versailles et de Trianon, Versailles, France. Copyright Réunion des Musées Nationaux/Art Resource, NY.)

❧

Chapter 2

THE FUTURE UNFOLDING IN AMERICA:

Alexis de Tocqueville,
Democracy in America (1835, 1840)

> I confess that in America I saw more than America; I sought there the image of democracy itself, with its inclinations, its character, its prejudices, and its passions, in order to learn what we have to fear or hope from its progress. (Vol. I, 14)

The single most cited book on American politics over the years may well be one written by a non-American. Since its publication in the mid-nineteenth century, Alexis de Tocqueville's *Democracy in America* has been widely acclaimed as one of the most important and perceptive analyses of American politics ever written. Tocqueville was, in fact, the first person to tackle the challenge of explaining the nature of American democracy and its larger meaning in world history. Although he was certainly not the first to perceive that the experiment unfolding in the United States represented a new chapter in world history, one with repercussions for the Old World, Tocqueville expounded on this theme with an unprecedented erudition and keen eye. Much of what he said about American democracy was complimentary, some of it was highly critical, but all of it reflected his conviction that what was developing in the United States was transformative for mankind.

Alexis de Tocqueville (1805–59) was a member of the French aristocracy, born when Napoleon I was Emperor of France. Although an aristocrat by birth, his politics were liberal in the nineteenth-century sense of that word. As an aristocrat, Tocqueville was far from being sentimental about the masses, nor was he an admirer of the values and preoccupations of the new aristocracy of commerce and manufacturing that was emerging on both sides of the Atlantic. He was a member of the French Chamber of Deputies between 1839 and 1848, supporting such reforms as

All references to *Democracy in America* in this book are from the Everyman's Library edition (Toronto: Alfred A. Knopf, 1994).

the decentralization of government and an independent judiciary. Throughout his lifetime, however, he never advocated the abolition of monarchy. During the European revolutions of 1848, brought on by economic crises and failed harvests that generated widespread misery among the masses, Tocqueville's sympathies were with the established forces of social order, in opposition to reforms that aimed to ameliorate the situation of the common people.

At the same time, however, he was passionate about liberty in the tradition of such great thinkers as Locke, Montesquieu, and Rousseau. Indeed, his love of individual freedom was the chief factor that led him to fear what he called the 'tyranny of the majority' and a sort of leveling uniformity in public opinion and intolerance of unorthodox views that he believed were characteristic of American democracy. Along with the authors of *The Federalist Papers*, Tocqueville put his faith in the US Constitution and its institutional arrangements to check the dangers to which liberty was subjected under American democracy.

When Tocqueville wrote *Democracy in America*, the disciplinary boundaries of modern intellectual life and the pigeonholes of academe did not yet exist. Tocqueville was a jurist by training, but he had the classical education typical of aristocrats of his time and also had studied European history and philosophy. *Democracy in America* combines aspects of these various influences into a *genre* that defies neat categorization. It is at the same time history, philosophy, political science, and sociology. Indeed, it is the sweep of Tocqueville's intellectual perspective and his persistent search for the broader significance of his observations for the human condition that—leaving aside the fact that he seems to have been right about so much of what he describes—account for the reputation of *Democracy in America* and the fact that it is still indispensable reading for serious students of American politics.

When Tocqueville visited the United States for the first and only time in 1831, democratic government was uncommon. Aristocracy was still the rule in the societies of the Old World, but, Tocqueville believed, it was fighting a losing battle. In his introduction to Volume I of *Democracy in America*, he writes:

> Gradually the distinctions of rank are done away with; the barriers that once severed mankind are falling; property is divided, power is shared by many, the light of intelligence spreads, and the capacities of all classes tend toward equality. Society becomes democratic, and the empire of

democracy is slowly and peaceably introduced into institutions and customs. (Vol. I, 9)

This historical tendency toward democracy he called an 'irresistible revolution' (ibid., 6), and thus he expected to see in America a foreshadowing of developments that his native France and other European countries would experience in time.

In some ways *Democracy in America* deserves to be read as a prophetic work. As such, it occupies a prominent place in a literature that extends from the Pilgrim Fathers of New England, who saw America as nothing short of a promised land, down to the present day. This is evident throughout *Democracy in America*, from Tocqueville's clearly stated belief that the future of Old World societies could be foreseen in the equality of social conditions that so struck him in the United States, his prescient remarks on how 'variety is disappearing from the human race' (Vol. II, 229)—what we might call 'Americanization' today—to his rather uncanny prophesying of the twentieth-century rivalry for global dominance between the United States and Russia (Vol. I, 434).

It is only a mild exaggeration to say that Tocqueville originated what would come to be known as the *end of history* school of American studies. By this I mean that he, and many others since him, have seen America's unique role in world history as breaking the trail to a form of civilization for which history provides no guide. In the last chapter of *Democracy in America* he states, 'I go back from age to age up to the remotest antiquity, but I find no parallel to what is occurring before my eyes' (Vol. II, 331). The rise of mass democracy was a phenomenon unknown to man, and one that Tocqueville believed represented a significant break from the history of what had gone before. Tocqueville would not have described this as 'progress', in any upward longitudinal sense of the word. He foresaw both opportunities and risks, and concludes *Democracy in America* on a somewhat uncertain and worried note.

When Tocqueville wrote his masterly analysis of American politics the United States was far from being a world power. Although the Monroe Doctrine (1823) had already warned the European powers that the American government would not tolerate Old World expansion of their existing territories in America's hemisphere, the military might of the fledgling republic was not particularly impressive. Economically, the United States neither exported very much to the rest of the world nor was it dependent on imports from other countries. It lagged behind England in terms of its level of industrialization and, unlike England, France, Spain, and even the Netherlands, it had no overseas network of possessions and economic tributaries.

Culturally, the picture was rather mixed. Although there were no American cultural exports to speak of—the rest of the world did not read American writers or admire her painters, sculptors, or poets—the *idea of America* was already powerful. For John Locke, America was the blank slate on which mankind would inscribe a new story of an egalitarian civilization. For religious dissidents, America represented the idea of freedom. For romantics like Rousseau and Chateaubriand, America represented the land of the 'noble savage', whom they believed to be uncorrupted by the customs, values, and institutions of civilization. For most of those who left the Old World for America during the seventeenth and eighteenth centuries, it represented escape from a society in which they had nothing and no prospects, to a place where they had at least the opportunity of doing better materially. Freedom, escape, opportunity, and noble innocence were already among the ideas associated with America. In coming to America, like any educated European of his time, Tocquevile brought with him an idea of what America represented. This idea was, on the whole, sympathetic, in the tradition of his countryman J. Hector St John de Crèvecoeur. Unlike a number of English visitors to America who wrote about their sojourns in the New World at about the same time, notably Charles Dickens and Mrs Trollope, Tocqueville was able to see beyond what must have appeared to a French aristocrat the sometimes rough-hewn manners and lack of Old World courtesies of Americans, to perceive a democratic culture that rejected servility and the recognition of social rank.

It is difficult to distill the hundreds of pages of *Democracy in America* into a handful of major conclusions. Nevertheless, in this work of enormous sweep and brilliant insight, several points are central to the author's perception of American politics and society.

1. THE EQUALITY OF SOCIAL CONDITIONS IN AMERICA UNDERPINS DEMOCRACY

Nothing struck Alexis de Tocqueville more forcibly than what he called the equality of social conditions in America. By this he did not mean that there were no inequalities in wealth or social status in America, but that these differences were much narrower than in Europe and, importantly, were not based on birth or some other ascriptive criterion. Although he never used the term, Tocqueville characterized the United States as the first middle-class society, a society in which the middle class was both preponderant in terms of size but also in terms of its influence on the manners and values of society.

In explaining the lack of class distinctions in America, Tocqueville stressed the role played by several factors. These included laws of inheritance and social origins.

Laws of inheritance. Tocqueville, like the founders of the American republic, was a firm believer in the importance of laws and institutions as regulators of social conduct and influences on politics. He observed that under American law of inheritance, the death of a property-owner resulted in the equal division of his property among his heirs. This is not to say that Americans were required by law to divide their property equally among their descendants, but that unlike the system of primogeniture that prevailed in most of Europe, the estate of a deceased property-holder did not automatically pass into the hands of his oldest male heir. The consequence of primogeniture, Tocqueville noted, was to keep property concentrated in relatively few hands and to reinforce an ascriptive notion of entitlement and social status. By contrast, the practice of equal partition of property guaranteed that wealth would circulate more broadly and rapidly. Moreover, because of the inevitability of property being divided among a number of heirs, the link between a family and a particular piece of land—the 'ancestral domain', as Tocqueville put it—is weakened and eventually severed. Consequently, he writes, 'wealth circulates with inconceivable rapidity, and experience shows that it is rare to find two succeeding generations in the full enjoyment of it' (Vol. I, 51).

Origins. Tocqueville attaches considerable importance to the character of the first immigrants to New England. 'The entire man', he argues, 'is to be seen in the cradle of the child' (Vol. I, 26). Early in Volume I of *Democracy in America* Tocqueville describes at some length the beliefs and institutions of those who settled what is now the northeast corner of the United States. It must be said that he has little to say about the society and culture of the South, aside from some observations about the colony of Virginia, seeming to imply that the different culture of that region— which he acknowledges was powerfully influenced by slavery—is less important to understanding the true character of the United States, and left very little mark on American political culture, compared to New England.

What struck Tocqueville about the social origins of Americans was a combination of the relative uniformity of their origins—most spoke the same language and came from the same country—and the fact that they came from the same stratum of society. As he says:

> The settlers who established themselves on the shores of New England all belonged to the more independent classes of their native country. Their union on the soil of America at once presented the singular phenomenon of a society containing neither lords nor common people, and we may almost say neither rich nor poor. These men possessed, in proportion to their number, a greater mass of intelligence than is to be found in any European nation of our time. (Vol. I, 31)

Moreover, those who settled New England, both the Puritans and those who left the Old World for reasons other than religious persecution, were familiar with liberal ideas that were already taking root in England. Tocqueville mentions 'the intervention of the people in public affairs, the free voting of taxes, the responsibility of the agents of power, personal liberty, and trial by jury' (Vol. I, 39) as principles that were well established in the New England colonies, though they had yet to triumph in any European country.

Democracy in America was written before the waves of Irish, German, and Eastern European immigration in the middle to late nineteenth century. It is difficult to know whether Tocqueville would have revised his assessment of the role played by the social origins of the Anglo-Americans if he had witnessed the huge influx of non-Anglo immigrants whom later commentators, like H.G. Wells, would consider a potential threat to the value system of the United States.[1] What is clear, however, is that Tocqueville believed the cultural baggage of the early immigrants to have been decisive in its impact on the political culture that developed in America. In words that anticipate the *fragment theory* developed by Harvard historian Louis Hartz over a century later, Tocqueville states:

> The emigrants who colonized the shores of America in the beginning of the seventeenth century somehow separated the democratic principle from all the other principles that it had to contend with in the old communities of Europe, and transplanted it alone to the New World. It has been able to spread in perfect freedom and peaceably to determine the character of the laws by influencing the manners of the country. (Vol. I, 13)

2. Sovereignty of the People

> The people reign in the American political world as the Deity does in the universe. They are the cause and the aim of all things; everything comes from them, and everything is absorbed in them. (Vol. I, 58)

In these words Tocqueville encapsulated what was for him, and in the context of his times, a startling and novel characteristic of American political life. France, of course, had experienced its own revolution of 1789, under the democratic banner of *liberté, égalité, et fraternité*, but the democratic ethos of the French Revolution was soon swamped in the Reign of Terror, the emperorship of Napoleon I, and the reinstatement of the monarchy. The idea of popular sovereignty, expressed in the preamble to the United States Constitution as 'We the people . . .', was still only a theoretical notion in Europe. Readers of Locke and Rousseau were familiar with such ideas, but they were nowhere to be found in practice.

Tocqueville discusses the principle of popular sovereignty early in Volume I of *Democracy in America*, making clear his belief that this is one of the keys to understanding American politics. Popular sovereignty and the will of the people are, he observes, no mere artifice or hypocrisy used by rulers to conceal their true motives and interests. Rather, he says, the principle is genuinely believed in by rulers and ruled alike, and public officials are never allowed to forget that whatever authority they wield derives from the people.

There is a point here that Tocqueville does not make explicit, but which is implied in what he writes about the sovereignty of the people in American political life, that is, that the idea of the state as something apart from and above the people did not exist in the United States. The covenants of the Pilgrim founders of New England, while entered into under the authority of the British Crown, Tocqueville sees as the prototype of an American notion of popular sovereignty that grounded public authority on popular consent. The state, according to this view, was nothing more than the legal and institutional expression of the popular will. It was in no way superior to or separate from the people, unlike in the Old World where the idea of the state was influenced by centuries of feudalism and absolutism that the movement toward democracy could not completely abolish.

During Tocqueville's visit to the United States, Andrew Jackson was President. Jackson's populist style did not impress Tocqueville, who described him as a 'slave of the majority' (Vol. I, 414). What did impress

Tocqueville, however, was the lack of servile deference shown by American citizens to their elected officials, from the President down. This, of course, continues to be true today. Presidents, and all lesser officials, create a distance between themselves and the people at their peril. When Ronald Reagan was asked the secret of his popularity he did not hesitate to attribute this to the fact that when many Americans looked at him they saw themselves. It is hard to imagine a François Mitterand or Jacques Chirac saying the same!

3. INDIVIDUALISM

In the early nineteenth century individualism was still a very young idea. In the Old World it was still an intellectual notion rather than a lived reality. Tocqueville found individualism to be a rather dangerous notion. In a passage that deserves quotation in full, he says:

> As social conditions become more equal, the number of persons increases who, although they are neither rich nor powerful enough to exercise any great influence over their fellows, have nevertheless acquired or retained sufficient education and fortune to satisfy their own wants. They owe nothing to any man, they expect nothing from any man; they acquire the habit of always considering themselves as standing alone, and they are apt to imagine that their whole destiny is in their own hands. Thus not only does democracy make every man forget his ancestors, but it hides his descendants and separates his contemporaries from him; it throws him back forever upon himself alone and threatens in the end to confine him entirely within the solitude of his own heart. (Vol. II, 99)

This fear sounds quite contemporary. The communitarian philosopher Charles Taylor describes the United States as the archetypical atomistic society, in which people are deluded into believing that they are the authors of their own fates and in which human dignity is inevitably corroded by the failure to recognize that self-esteem and the experience of authentic meaning in one's life depend on others, or, in a word, on the ties of community. What has been praised by some as 'rugged individualism', and credited with the achievement of great things for both individuals *and* society, has been blamed by others for encouraging a dog-eat-dog mentality that is the antithesis of a truly civilized society.

Tocqueville was no great admirer of individualism. He would have been horrified by the idea of a society built around the nuclear family or the ethos of the so-called 'me generation'. Like Karl Marx after him, he believed individualism to be a dangerous sort of false consciousness. But unlike Marx he believed the threat that individualism posed to community could be neutralized in a society in which people cooperated with their neighbors to accomplish shared goals. In other words, Tocqueville believed that as long as individuals were willing to come together to achieve jointly what they would not be capable of individually, and without depending on the state, they could overcome the dangers of individualism.

4. CIVIL SOCIETY

The dangers of individualism, which Tocqueville believed to be great, were kept in check by several characteristics of American society. One of these involved the willingness of Americans to join together in common enterprises to achieve shared goals without relying on the state. 'As soon as several of the inhabitants of the United States have taken up an opinion or feeling which they wish to promote in the world,' he observes, 'they look out for mutual assistance; and as soon as they have found one another out, they combine. From that moment they are no longer isolated men' (Vol. II, 109). This tendency to associate with others of like mind and similar interests seemed to come naturally to Americans, Tocqueville observed. Enterprises that in the Old World would be undertaken and directed by the state or a person of wealth and social prominence were commonly the business of private voluntary associations in the United States. In this way were bonds of community forged between individuals and, moreover, citizens acquired the habit of looking to their own efforts and resources to get things done (what a later generation of social scientists would refer to as a sense of external efficacy).

It should be remembered that when *Democracy in America* was written, the prevailing view in the Old World was that centralized government and a strong state were necessary conditions for the accomplishment of great things. Tocqueville believed that this was true in matters of war and peace, and felt that the American political system was definitely inferior to that of France or Britain in this respect. But he saw that a weak state did not necessarily mean an enfeebled body politic. On the contrary, in America he saw a strong civil society that compensated for the weakness of the state. He probably would not have agreed with Henry David

Thoreau's words a generation later, to the effect that the American government never accomplished or hastened any useful undertaking except through the alacrity with which it got out of the way, but he saw that the strength of America's associational life—civil society—was a distinctive feature of American political life and one that helped generate bonds of community in a society that exalted the individual.

This argument has a very familiar ring to contemporary ears. Americans have often been described as a nation of joiners whose voluntary associations play a crucial role in linking citizens to one another and to the political process. Almond and Verba's characterization of the American civic culture recognizes the importance of associations to American democracy, and recent writings, like those of Robert Putnam, argue that the declining participation of Americans in these associations has contributed to the erosion of a sense of community and a rise in precisely the corrosive individualism that Tocqueville feared.[2]

The free institutions through which Americans governed their local affairs, according to Tocqueville, were another source of the strength of civil society in America. He noted that the general affairs of the United States engaged the attention and required the direct involvement of only the leading politicians, but that the local affairs that mattered to the day-to-day lives of citizens—roads, public works, schools, police protection, etc.—were attended to by the residents of local communities. Townhall democracy was one of the important ways in which Americans were reminded that they lived in communities and that individual interests must sometimes be compromised to serve the greater good.

Townhall democracy is, for the most part, a quaint anachronism in contemporary America. But although the experience of getting together in the local town hall or community center to debate and vote on community matters is no longer common, the participatory ethos expressed through such practices has survived in new forms. The greater frequency that Americans have to vote for public officials—from President to county drain commissioners—is one factor that keeps alive what might be described as a sense of citizen empowerment. But another, possibly more important factor is the culture of public opinion polling.

In no other country has public opinion polling been an important vehicle for gauging public preferences for so long and nowhere is the practice as deeply entrenched in the political system. Polling, at one level, represents an extension of the delegate model of political representation and decision-making and a rejection of the Burkean notion of the politician as trustee. It is an essentially populist practice, based as it is on the premise that the best way to govern is to ascertain as accurately as possible the preferences of the people and then translate these preferences into policies and government actions. The town hall of nineteenth-century New England becomes the virtual town hall of the latest Gallup or *Time*/CNN poll, complemented by the simulated experience of direct democracy represented by the electronic townhall meeting, televised or conducted in real time over the Internet.

5. MATERIALISM

The world knew excesses of wealth and its ostentatious displays before America. Newspaper publisher William Randolph Hearst's Xanadu and the opulent lifestyles immortalized in F. Scott Fitzgerald's *The Great Gatsby* might be considered modest alongside the obscene riches and luxuries of some of the Old World's aristocrats and potentates. But what was different about America, Tocqueville observed, was that the desire to acquire wealth was so widespread in the population. 'I never met in America', he writes, 'any citizens so poor as not to cast a glance of hope and envy on the enjoyments of the rich or whose imagination did not possess itself by anticipation of those good things that fate still obstinately withheld from him' (Vol. II, 129).

Americans of all economic ranks, Tocqueville maintained, shared what he called a 'passion for physical well-being' that derived from that fact that the United States was predominantly a middle-class society in which relatively few people could rest assured in the permanence of their wealth and in which few had reason to believe that their poverty was a permanent condition of their lives and those of their children. Even among those Americans who had already amassed great fortunes—and some already were to be found Tocqueville's time—the desire to acquire more and the fear of loss remained alive. Tocqueville explains this by noting that 'most of these wealthy persons were once poor; they have felt the sting of want; they were long prey to adverse fortunes; and now that the victory is won, the passions which accompanied the contest have survived it' (Vol. II, 129–30).

It is clear that Tocqueville thought that the materialism he observed in American society was a mixed blessing. He saw that the universal desire to better one's lot was responsible for improvement in the physical well-being of individuals and communities. But at the same time he worried about what might be described as the consequences for men's souls of acquisitiveness and a preoccupation with material well-being. He writes:

Their taste for physical gratifications must be regarded as the original source of that secret disquietude which the actions of the Americans betray and of that inconstancy of which they daily afford fresh examples.

He who has set his heart exclusively upon the pursuit of worldly welfare is always in a hurry, for he has but a limited time at his disposal to reach, to grasp, and to enjoy it. The recollection of the shortness of life is a constant spur to him. Besides the good things that he possesses, he every instant fancies a thousand others that death will prevent him from trying if he does not try them soon. This thought fills him with anxiety, fear, and regret and keeps his mind in ceaseless trepidation, which leads him perpetually to change his plans and his abode. (Vol. II, 137)

The abundance and prosperity that characterized American society, and which were widely distributed across that society, were accompanied by a restlessness and unease that Tocqueville attributed to the paradoxical effects of equality. 'When inequality of conditions is the common law of society,' he observes, 'the most marked inequalities do not strike the eye; when everything is nearly on the same level, the slightest differences are marked enough to hurt it. Hence the desire of equality always becomes more insatiable in proportion as equality is more complete' (Vol. II, 138). Thus it is that men and women who, by any objective standard, are well off continue to be restless to acquire more, ever conscious that someone possesses more than themselves and anxious that they not lose ground in the unceasing race to 'succeed' and 'get ahead' (terms that reflect the materialism and restlessness that Tocqueville observed).

This preoccupation with what we today might call getting and spending was bad for the soul, Tocqueville argued. Not only did it tend to encourage men to pursue false gods but, he believed, it also was responsible for mental illness! Tocqueville speaks of 'That strange melancholy which often haunts the inhabitants of democratic countries in the midst of their abundance', their occasional and irrational 'disgust at life', and even insanity (Vol. II, 139). These, he felt, could be attributed to a spiritually barren and psychologically unhealthy preoccupation with worldly things.

Tocqueville also feared that in a materialist society in which people are engrossed in their private affairs, there is the danger that public affairs may fall into the hands of a few, while the masses remain inattentive and indifferent to all but their private concerns. This was not the case in the United States, he argued. On the contrary, Americans seemed able and willing to give to public affairs the same effort and attention they devoted to private matters. This, he believed, was because Americans' sense of civic duty was influenced by their particular conception of the role of government, a conception of which John Locke would have approved. '[Americans] believe', said Tocqueville, 'that their chief business is to secure for themselves a government which will not debar them from the peaceful enjoyment of those possessions which they have already acquired' (Vol. II, 142). And of those that they hope to acquire, he might have added! Such a government cannot be expected if citizens feel no responsibility to partake in public affairs.

CONCLUSION

If *Democracy in America* is still standard reading for university courses on American Politics in the United States, which it is, the reason is not simply that much of what Alexis de Tocqueville says about his subject is flattering. The explanation has far more to do with the continuing relevance of his insights into American politics. One is constantly struck by the contemporary sound of so many of his observations on the traits of Americans and the nature of their politics. His fears about the corrosive effects of individualism and materialism and about the tyranny of public opinion all find contemporary echoes. His description of the middle-class ethos and egalitarianism of manners in the United States would probably be agreed to by most. And the importance of equality in social conditions for the maintenance of democracy now seems self-evidently true, although some today would argue that this equality no longer exists in sufficient degree to guarantee democratic government.

At the same time it must be said that Tocqueville visited the United States before the great expansion of settlement in the West of the country and the annexation of Texas. He did not travel further west than the region around Detroit and he spent very little time in the South. One might argue that the America he observed was rather incomplete and has become very different as a result of immigration, economic development, technology, and the history that has unfolded since his time. All of this is true, but it is also the case that *Democracy in America* would not occupy its undisputed place among the major interpretations of American politics were it not for the fact that it resonates with relevance for the understanding of America today, not just in Tocqueville's time.

Excerpts from Alexis de Tocqueville, *Democracy in America*

The Principle of the Sovereignty of the People in America

Whenever the political laws of the United States are to be discussed, it is with the doctrine of the sovereignty of the people that we must begin.

The principle of the sovereignty of the people, which is always to be found, more or less, at the bottom of almost all human institutions, generally remains there concealed from view. It is obeyed without being recognized, or if for a moment it is brought to light, it is hastily cast back into the gloom of the sanctuary.

'The will of the nation' is one of those phrases, that have been most largely abused by the wily and the despotic of every age. Some have seen the expression of it in the purchased suffrages of a few of the satellites of power; others, in the votes of a timid or an interested minority; and some have even discovered it in the silence of a people, on the supposition that the fact of submission established the right to command.

In America the principle of the sovereignty of the people is neither barren nor concealed, as it is with some other nations; it is recognized by the customs and proclaimed by the laws; it spreads freely, and arrives without impediment at its most remote consequences. If there is a country in the world where the doctrine of the sovereignty of the people can be fairly appreciated, where it can be studied in its application to the affairs of society, and where its dangers and its advantages may be judged, that country is assuredly America. (Vol. I, 55)

At the present day the principle of the sovereignty of the people has acquired in the United States all the practical development that the imagination can conceive. It is unencumbered by those fictions that are thrown over it in other countries, and it appears in every possible form, according to the exigency of the occasion. Sometimes the laws are made by the people in a body, as at Athens; and sometimes its representatives, chosen by universal suffrage, transact business in its name and under its immediate supervision.

In some countries a power exists which, though it is in a degree foreign to the social body, directs it, and forces it to pursue a certain track. In others the ruling force is divided, being partly within and partly without the ranks of the people. But nothing of the kind is to be seen in the United States; there society governs itself for itself. All power centers in its bosom, and scarcely an individual is to be met with who would venture to conceive or, still less, to express the idea of seeking it elsewhere. The nation participates in the making of its laws by the choice of its legislators, and in the execution of them by the choice of the agents of the executive government, it may almost be said to govern itself, so feeble and so restricted is the share left to the administration, so little do the authorities forget their popular origin and the power from which they emanate. The people reign in the American political world as the Deity does in the universe. They are the cause and the aim of all things; everything comes from them, and everything is absorbed in them. (Vol. I, 57–8)

SOCIAL CONDITION OF THE ANGLO-AMERICANS

It is not only the fortunes of men that are equal in America; even their acquirements partake in some degree of the same uniformity. I do not believe that there is a country in the world where, in proportion to the population, there are so few ignorant and at the same time so few learned individuals. Primary instruction is within the reach of everybody; superior instruction is scarcely to be obtained by any. This is not surprising; it is, in fact, the necessary consequence of what I have advanced above. Almost all the Americans are in easy circumstances and can therefore obtain the first elements of human knowledge.

In America there are but few wealthy persons; nearly all Americans have to take a profession. Now, every profession requires an apprenticeship. The Americans can devote to general education only the early years of life. At fifteen they enter upon their calling, and thus their education generally ends at the age when ours begins. If it is continued beyond that point, it aims only towards a particular specialized and profitable purpose; one studies science as one takes up a business; and one takes up only those applications whose immediate practicality is recognized.

In America most of the rich men were formerly poor; most of those who now enjoy leisure were absorbed in business during their youth; the consequence of this is that when they might have had a taste for study, they had no time for it, and when the time is at their disposal, they have no longer the inclination.

There is no class, then, in America, in which the taste for intellectual pleasures is transmitted with hereditary fortune and leisure and by which the labors of the intellect are held in honor. Accordingly, there is an equal want of the desire and the power of application to these objects.

A middling standard is fixed in America for human knowledge. All approach as near to it as they can; some as they rise, others as they descend. Of course, a multitude of persons are to be found who entertain the same number of ideas on religion, history, science, political economy, legislation, and government. The gifts of intellect proceed directly from God, and man cannot prevent their unequal distribution. But it is at least a consequence of what I have just said that although the capacities of men are different, as the Creator intended they should be, the means that Americans find for putting them to use are equal.

In America the aristocratic element has always been feeble from its birth; and if at the present day it is not actually destroyed, it is at any rate so completely disabled that we can scarcely assign to it any degree of influence on the course of affairs.

The democratic principle, on the contrary, has gained so much strength by time, by events, and by legislation, as to have become not only predominant, but all-powerful. No family or corporate authority can be perceived; very often one cannot even discover in it any very lasting individual influence.

America, then, exhibits in her social state an extraordinary phenomenon. Men are there seen on a greater equality in point of fortune and intellect, or, in other words, more equal in their strength, than in any other country of the world, or in any age of which history has preserved the remembrance. (Vol. I, 51–3)

HOW EQUALITY SUGGESTS TO AMERICANS THE IDEA OF THE INDEFINITE PERFECTIBILITY OF MAN

Equality suggests to the human mind several ideas that would not have originated from any other source, and it modifies almost all those previously entertained. I take as an example the idea of human perfectibility, because it is one of the principal notions that the intellect can conceive and because it constitutes of itself a great philosophical theory, which is everywhere to be traced by its consequences in the conduct of human affairs.

Although man has many points of resemblance with the brutes, one trait is peculiar to himself: he improves; they are incapable of improvement. Mankind could not fail to discover this difference from the beginning. The idea of perfectibility is therefore as old as the world; equality did not give birth to it, but has imparted to it a new character.

When the citizens of a community are classed according to rank, profession, or birth and when all men are forced to follow the career which chance has opened before them, everyone thinks that the utmost limits of human power are to be discerned in proximity to himself, and no one seeks any longer to resist the inevitable law of his destiny. Not, indeed, that an aristocratic people absolutely deny man's faculty of self-improvement, but they do not hold it to be indefinite; they can conceive amelioration, but not change: they imagine that the future condition of society may be better, but not essentially different; and, while they admit that humanity has made progress and may still have some to make, they assign to it beforehand certain impassable limits.

Thus they do not presume that they have arrived at the supreme good or at absolute truth (what people or what man was ever wild enough to imagine it?), but they cherish an opinion that they have pretty nearly reached that degree of greatness and knowledge which our imperfect nature admits of; and as nothing moves about them, they are willing to fancy that everything is in its fit place. Then it is that the legislator affects to lay down eternal laws; that kings and nations will raise none but imperishable monuments; and that the present generation undertakes to spare generations to come the care of regulating their destinies.

In proportion as castes disappear and the classes of society draw together, as manners, customs, and laws vary, because of the tumultuous intercourse of men, and new facts arise, as new truths are brought to light, as ancient opinions are dissipated and others take their place, the image of an ideal but always fugitive perfection presents itself to the human mind. Continual changes are then every instant occurring under the observation of every man; the position of some is rendered worse, and he learns but too well that no people and no individual, however enlightened they may be, can lay claim to infallibility; the condition of others is improved, whence he infers that man is endowed with an indefinite faculty for improvement. His reverses teach him that none have discovered absolute good; his success stimulates him to the never ending pursuit of it. Thus, forever seeking, forever falling to rise again, often disappointed, but not discouraged, he tends unceasingly towards that unmeasured greatness so indistinctly visible at the end of the long track which humanity has yet to tread.

It can hardly be believed how many facts naturally flow from the philosophical theory of the indefinite perfectibility of man or how strong an influence it exercises even on those who, living entirely for the purposes of action and not of thought, seem to conform their actions to it without knowing anything about it.

I accost an American sailor and inquire why the ships of his country are built so as to last for only a short time; he answers without hesitation that the art of navigation is every day making such rapid progress that the finest vessel would become almost useless if it lasted beyond a few years. In these words, which fell accidentally, and on a particular subject, from an uninstructed man, I recognize the general and systematic idea upon which a great people direct all their concerns.

Aristocratic nations are naturally too liable to narrow the scope of human perfectibility; democratic nations, to expand it beyond reason. (Vol. II, 33–4)

PATRIOTISM OF AMERICANS

How does it happen that in the United States, where the inhabitants have only recently immigrated to the land which they now occupy, and brought neither customs nor traditions with them there; where they meet one another for the first time with no previous acquaintance; where, in short, the instinctive love of country can scarcely exist; how does it happen that everyone takes as zealous an interest in the affairs of his township, his county, and the whole state as if they were his own? It is because everyone, in his sphere, takes an active part in the government of society.

The lower orders in the United States understand the influence exercised by the general prosperity upon their own welfare; simple as this observation is, it is too rarely made by the people. Besides, they are accustomed to regard this prosperity as the fruit of their own exertions. The citizen looks upon the fortune of the public as his own, and he labors for the good of the state, not merely from a sense of pride or duty, but from what I venture to term cupidity.

It is unnecessary to study the institutions and the history of the Americans in order to know the truth of this remark, for their manners render it sufficiently evident. As the American participates in all that is done in his country, he thinks himself obliged to defend whatever may be censured in it; for it is not only his country that is then attacked, it is himself. The consequence is that his national pride resorts to a thousand artifices and descends to all the petty tricks of personal vanity.

Nothing is more embarrassing in the ordinary intercourse of life than this irritable patriotism of the Americans. A stranger may be well inclined to praise many of the institutions of their country, but he begs permission to blame some things in it, a permission that is inexorably refused. America is therefore a free country in which, lest anybody should be hurt by your remarks, you are not allowed to speak freely of private individuals or of the state, of the citizens or of the authorities, of public or of private undertakings, or, in short, of anything at all except, perhaps, the climate and the soil; and even then Americans will be found ready to defend both as if they had co-operated in producing them. (Vol. I, 243–4)

POWER EXERCISED BY THE MAJORITY IN AMERICA UPON OPINION

It is in the examination of the exercise of thought in the United States that we clearly perceive how far the power of the majority surpasses all the powers with which we are acquainted in Europe. Thought is an invisible and subtle power that mocks all the efforts of tyranny. At the present time the most absolute monarchs in Europe cannot prevent certain opinions hostile to their authority from circulating in secret through their dominions and even in their courts. It is not so in America; as long as the majority is still undecided, discussion is carried on; but as soon as its decision is irrevocably pronounced, everyone is silent, and the friends as well as the opponents of the measure unite in assenting to its propriety. The reason for this is perfectly clear: no monarch is so absolute as to combine all the powers of society in his own hands and to conquer all opposition, as a majority is able to do, which has the right both of making and of executing the laws.

The authority of a king is physical and controls the actions of men without subduing their will. But the majority possesses a power that is physical and moral at the same time, which acts upon the will as much as upon the actions and represses not only all contest, but all controversy.

I know of no country in which there is so little independence of mind and real freedom of discussion as in America. In any constitutional state in

Europe every sort of religious and political theory may be freely preached and disseminated; for there is no country in Europe so subdued by any single authority as not to protect the man who raises his voice in the cause of truth from the consequences of his hardihood. If he is unfortunate enough to live under an absolute government, the people are often on his side; if he inhabits a free country, he can, if necessary, find a shelter behind the throne. The aristocratic part of society supports him in some countries, and the democracy in others. But in a nation where democratic institutions exist, organized like those of the United States, there is but one authority, one element of strength and success, with nothing beyond it. (Vol. I, 263)

TYRANNY OF THE MAJORITY

In my opinion, the main evil of the present democratic institutions of the United States does not arise, as is often asserted in Europe, from their weakness, but from their irresistible strength. I am not so much alarmed at the excessive liberty which reigns in that country as at the inadequate securities which one finds there against tyranny.

When an individual or a party is wronged in the United States, to whom can he apply for redress? If to public opinion, public opinion constitutes the majority; if to the legislature, it represents the majority and implicitly obeys it; if to the executive power, it is appointed by the majority and serves as a passive tool in its hands. The public force consists of the majority under arms; the jury is the majority invested with the right of hearing judicial cases; and in certain states even the judges are elected by the majority. However iniquitous or absurd the measure of which you complain, you must submit to it as well as you can.

If, on the other hand, a legislative power could be so constituted as to represent the majority without necessarily being the slave of its passions, an executive so as to retain a proper share of authority, and a judiciary so as to remain independent of the other two powers, a government would be formed which would still be democratic while incurring scarcely any risk of tyranny. (Vol. I, 260–1)

PUBLIC ASSOCIATIONS IN CIVIL LIFE

Feelings and opinions are recruited, the heart is enlarged, and the human mind is developed only by the reciprocal influence of men upon one another. I have shown that these influences are almost null in democratic countries; they must therefore be artificially created, and this can only be accomplished by associations.

When the members of an aristocratic community adopt a new opinion or conceive a new sentiment, they give it a station, as it were, beside themselves, upon the lofty platform where they stand; and opinions or sentiments so conspicuous to the eyes of the multitude are easily introduced into the minds or hearts of all around. In democratic countries the governing power alone is naturally in a condition to act in this manner, but it is easy to see that its action is always inadequate, and often dangerous. A government can no more be competent to keep alive and to renew the circulation of opinions and feelings among a great people than to manage all the speculations of productive industry. No sooner does a government attempt to go beyond its political sphere and to enter upon this new track than it exercises, even unintentionally, an insupportable tyranny; for a government can only dictate strict rules, the opinions which it favors are rigidly enforced, and it is never easy to discriminate between its advice and its commands. Worse still will be the case if the government really believes itself interested in preventing all circulation of ideas; it will then stand motionless and oppressed by the heaviness of voluntary torpor. Governments, therefore, should not be the only active powers; associations ought, in democratic nations, to stand in lieu of those powerful private individuals whom the equality of conditions has swept away.

As soon as several of the inhabitants of the United States have taken up an opinion or a feeling which they wish to promote in the world, they look out for mutual assistance; and as soon as they have found one another out, they combine. From that moment they are no longer isolated men, but a power seen from afar, whose actions serve for an example and whose language is listened to. (Vol. II, 108-9)

OF THE TASTE FOR PHYSICAL WELL-BEING IN AMERICA

Among a nation where aristocracy predominates in society and keeps it stationary, the people in the end get as much accustomed to poverty as the rich to their opulence. The latter bestow no anxiety on their physical comforts because they enjoy them without an effort; the former do not think of things which they despair of obtaining and which they hardly know enough of to desire. In communities of this kind the imagination of the poor is driven to seek another world, the miseries of real life enclose it, but it escapes from their control and flies to seek its pleasures far beyond.

When, on the contrary, the distinctions of ranks are obliterated and privileges are destroyed, when hereditary property is subdivided and education and freedom are widely diffused, the desire of acquiring the comforts of the world haunts the imagination of the poor, and the dread of losing them that of the rich. Many scanty fortunes spring up; those who possess them have a sufficient share of physical gratifications to conceive a taste for these pleasures, not enough to satisfy it. They never procure them without exertion, and they never indulge in them without apprehension. They are therefore always straining to pursue or to retain gratifications so delightful, so imperfect, so fugitive.

If I were to inquire what passion is most natural to men who are stimulated and circumscribed by the obscurity of their birth or the mediocrity of their fortune, I could discover none more peculiarly appropriate to their condition than this love of physical prosperity. The passion for physical comforts is essentially a passion of the middle classes; with those classes it grows and spreads, with them it is preponderant. From them it mounts into the higher orders of society and descends into the mass of the people.

I never met in America any citizen so poor as not to cast a glance of hope and envy on the enjoyments of the rich or whose imagination did not possess itself by anticipation of those good things that fate still obstinately withheld from him. (Vol. II, 129)

Selected Writings on Alexis de Tocqueville and *Democracy in America*

The literature on Tocqueville and *Democracy in America* is vast. The following works represent a mere handful of that which is available to readers who wish to know more about America's most celebrated foreign observer.

A.S. Eisenstadt, ed., *Tocqueville's Democracy in America Reconsidered*, New Brunswick, NJ: Transaction Publishers, 1988. This is a contemporary collection of essays on Tocqueville and his writings.

André Jardin, *Tocqueville*. New York: Farrar Strauss Giroux, 1988. This biography is widely considered to be one of the best.

Richard Reeves, *American Journey: Travelling with Tocqueville in Search of Democracy in America*. New York: Simon and Schuster, 1982. This is a very readable account of Tocqueville's journey in America, written by an American journalist.

L.A. Siedentop, *Tocqueville*. Oxford: Oxford University Press, 1994. One of the many standard analyses of the Frenchman's ideas.

The Tocqueville Review, published by the Tocqueville Society, Charlottesville, Virginia. This scholarly journal, published since 1979, is devoted to Tocqueville and the questions that arise from his writings.

FIRST IMPRESSIONS.

Pres. R-s-v-l-t. "My! if he ain't just a daisy! Most attractive personal'ty, I do declare! Hope I shan't get kind er hitched up in them eyebrow 'rrangements!"

Prof. Br-ce. "H'm! nice pleasant expression. One who was not a purist in language might almost describe him as a '*peach*.' Development of the teeth suggests tenacity and strength of character. Well, well! we must try to avoid them!"

This cartoon from *Punch* portrays the first meeting between James Bryce, then Britain's ambassador to the United States, and President Theodore Roosevelt (1907). (*By permission of the Punch Cartoon Library and Archive, London.*)

Chapter 3

❧

THE CAREFUL EMPIRICIST:

James Bryce,
The American Commonwealth (1888)

James Bryce's *The American Commonwealth* was published over 50 years after *Democracy in America*, and was written very consciously in the shadow of Tocqueville's monumental work. Like Tocqueville, Bryce realized that his subject was nothing less than the future of mankind and that the society taking shape in the United States—the Land of the Future, as he called it—would have consequences far beyond the shores of America. And like Tocqueville he produced a sprawling interpretation of American politics that moves back and forth between detailed observation and broad generalization.

But James Bryce (1838–1922) set out to do something rather different from Alexis de Tocqueville, approaching the subject in a different spirit and with a different method. Bryce explains these differences at the outset of *The American Commonwealth*, aware that his readers would inevitably make comparisons between his book and Tocqueville's masterpiece. He writes:

> To De Tocqueville, America was primarily a democracy, the ideal democracy, fraught with lessons for Europe, and above all for his own France. What he has given us is not so much a description of the country and people as a treatise, full of fine observation and elevated thinking, upon democracy, a treatise whose conclusions are illustrated from America, but are founded, not so much on an analysis of American phenomena, as on general and somewhat speculative views of democracy which the circumstances of France had suggested. (4)

Tocqueville, he is saying, interpreted the American experience through the lens of a philosopher-historian, concerned to discover what lessons it

---

All references to *The American Commonwealth* in this book are from the Capricorn Books abridged edition (New York: G.P. Putnam's Sons, 1959).

might hold for the Old World and, in particular, his native France. The Frenchman's method was deductive and philosophical, based on a theory of democracy that he found illustrated in the American case and which, in a sense, he imposed on the institution, behaviors, and values he observed in the United States. Bryce did not intend this as a criticism of Tocqueville's magisterial interpretation of American democracy, but rather as a warning to his readers that his own intention was not to write a work of philosophy in the style of Tocqueville.

What Bryce produced instead was a first-rate work of empirical analysis that, while it lacks the philosophical sweep of *Democracy in America*, is clearly superior to Tocqueville's work in terms of its description and analysis of the institutions and norms of American politics. Bryce was a clear-thinking social scientist who described his method this way: 'My own plan has been to write down what struck me as the salient and dominant facts, and then to test, by consulting American friends and by a further study of American books, the views which I had reached' (8). He visited the United States on three separate occasions before writing *The American Commonwealth*, seeing more of the country than had Tocqueville and, like Tocqueville, talking with innumerable people from all walks of life, including some of the most prominent men in American public and intellectual life.

His elite connections and intellectual reputation guaranteed Bryce's entree into the company of some of the best and the brightest of America. Bryce had been a brilliant student at university, writing *The Holy Roman Empire* when he was only 25 and being named to the prestigious Regius Chair of Civil Law at Oxford when he was 32. Like Tocqueville, he combined his intellectual pursuits with political activity, sitting in the British House of Commons for over 20 years, holding various cabinet positions, serving as British ambassador to the United States between 1907 and 1913, and finally entering the House of Lords on his return to England. And like Tocqueville, it is fair to say that Bryce was a liberal with upperclass sympathies, but who was in no way repelled by what he saw of the masses in America. Neither the liberal aristocrat Tocqueville nor the liberal intellectual Bryce painted a picture of 'mob-ocracy' in America, although this was not an uncommon portrayal of American politics among European visitors to America.

Bryce wrote about the United States because of his conviction that America represented 'an experiment in the rule of the multitude, tried on a scale unprecedentedly vast, and the results of which everyone is concerned to watch' (1). The reason for this concern, he wrote, was that this experiment was 'believed to disclose and display the type of institutions towards which, as a law of fate, the rest of civilized mankind are forced to move' (1). This is the prophetic wavelength that is perhaps the defining feature of *Democracy in America*. But it is not the defining characteristic in Bryce's work. Although he shared with Tocqueville and many others the conviction that America was the future unfolding, he wanted to write a dispassionate description of the American political scene, untainted by philosophical speculations and partisan prejudice. Indeed, he says early on in *The American Commonwealth* that '[t]he social and political experiments of America constantly cited in Europe both as patterns and as warnings are hardly ever cited with due knowledge of the facts, much less with comprehension of what they teach' (2). Bryce wished to rectify this failing.

The landscape of America, compared to Tocqueville's time, was significantly different when Bryce visited. The country had undergone the Civil War, of course, and slavery had been legally abolished. But in other ways, too, the United States was significantly different from the country that Tocqueville had observed.

To begin with, the population had increased about fourfold, from roughly 15 million to 60 million. A significant part of this increase was due to immigration from 'non-traditional' sources, including large numbers of Irish, German, Slavic, and Jewish descent. America was still dominated by those of Anglo-Saxon background, but the great American melting pot was now beginning to stew with the addition of previously unfamiliar elements. The challenge of integrating these elements into American society and their impact on American politics were not questions to which Tocqueville devoted much attention, but virtually all serious analyses of America from the latter half of the nineteenth century to the present day have had to deal with these issues.

Territorially, the United States had reached its full continental dimensions by the time Bryce visited, and he traveled to far more of it than did Tocqueville, reaching the west coast of the United States. Alaska had been purchased from Russia, the idea of Manifest Destiny had been born, and the prospect of free or very inexpensive land was drawing millions of people west of the Mississippi.

Militarily, the United States was no longer in any danger from European powers. The settlement of the western territories and their gradual rise to statehood, the end of British colonies on the northern border when Canada became independent in 1867, and the declining power of Spain in Latin America left the United States without any serious threats to its territory and people.

Economically, the United States was on the cusp of becoming the world's economic powerhouse when *The American Commonwealth* was written. Bryce was not an economist, and although he spends time talking about Wall Street, the railroads, and the emergence of great fortunes in the United States—the era of plutocrats and robber barons was beginning—he says little about the place of the American economy in the world. It was, however, already the single largest economy in the world by the end of the nineteenth century.

This is the context of Bryce's observations, a context that was different in some important ways from the time in which Tocqueville's interpretation was situated. Notwithstanding these changes, what might be described as the chief lineaments of American society were largely the same and the conclusions that Bryce arrives at regarding the character of Americans and their politics, and the explanations he offers for these, are in many important ways similar to those of Tocqueville.

The enduring parts of *The American Commonwealth* that echo with relevance today are those that deal with political culture. Like Tocqueville before him, Bryce was fascinated by the contrast between the Old and New Worlds in matters of manners and mores, and their impact on political life. Among these points of contrast the following stand out.

1. PUBLIC OPINION

Bryce devotes an entire long section of *The American Commonwealth*, comprised of several chapters, to an analysis of public opinion in the United States. He believed that it held the key to understanding American democracy. 'In no country is public opinion so powerful as in the United States,' he writes, '[and] in no country can it be so well studied' (280). Bryce argues that public opinion, understood as the beliefs, attitudes, and preferences of the general population, has always been 'the chief and ultimate power in nearly all nations at nearly all times' (288). There is, however, a dramatic difference between the role of public opinion in the aristocratic monarchies and oligarchies that have been the rule through most of human history and its role in a mass democracy: 'in the former the people instinctively obey a power which they do not know to be really their own creation, and to stand by their own permission; whereas in the latter the people feel their supremacy, and consciously treat their rulers as their agents, while the rulers obey a power which they admit to have made and to be able to unmake them—the popular will' (290). This sounds a lot like Tocqueville when he talks about the sovereignty of the people in America. It also calls to mind the now familiar distinction that Gabriel Almond and Sidney Verba made, in their classic cross-national study of democracy, *The Civic Culture*, between *subject* and *participant* political culture. In the former the mass of people view their relationship to the state and those who exercise public authority as a passive one: their disposition vis-à-vis public office-holders is deferential. In the latter case, however, members of the general population display a more active demeanor toward the state and those who hold public office. They are more likely to think that their views matter and should be listened to, and less likely to retreat into quiet compliance in the face of laws and state actions that they object to.

Where citizens expect that politicians should and will take their ideas and preferences seriously, and are unwilling to assume that political or other elites have some special knowledge or wisdom to which 'common folk' should defer, public opinion is a force to be reckoned with in politics. This was the situation that Bryce observed, and which he noted was one of the most remarkable differences between American and English democracy. Not only were politicians in America forced to follow public opinion more often than lead it, but that other important class of opinion-makers, journalists, was also in thrall to the opinions of the masses. Bryce's explanation of this has a very contemporary resonance. He attributed the general similarity of journalists' views and public opinion to the fact that the newspapers were privately owned enterprises with, in his words, 'their circulation to consider' (286). Their owners were loath to see them take a political line that might jeopardize their sales and profitability. *Plus ça change, plus c'est la même chose!*

A study of the role of public opinion in European compared to American democracy showed, Bryce argued, that in the Old World 'The Constitution has become democratic, [but] the habits of the nation are still aristocratic' (287). The conclusions that he drew from this were rather different from those drawn by Tocqueville, who was equally struck by the significance of public opinion in America. Tocqueville believed that one aspect of American democracy, indeed, perhaps the most disagreeable and dangerous aspect, was what he characterized as the too-often crushing and conformist weight of public opinion. One of his most famous and least flattering observations about America was that in no country was independent thought so stifled and freedom of discussion so rare. Within the limits of the conventional wisdom and mainstream public opinion all was permitted. Outside this circle a politician, journalist, or writer could only expect ostracism and failure. Public opinion was, Tocqueville felt, one of the chief means through which the tyranny of the majority operated.

Bryce simply did not agree with this very negative assessment of the impact of public opinion on American public life. He doubted that majority opinion was as actively coercive as Tocqueville maintained and went on to say that, even assuming this to have been true when Tocqueville visited America, it was no longer a fair characterization of public opinion 50 years later. Indeed, Bryce argued that public opinion in the United States—as he observed it—was actually quite tolerant, a fact he attributed to the greater maturity of American society than in Tocqueville's time and the healthy separation of matters of religion from politics. 'Taking the country all in all,' Bryce writes, 'it is hard to imagine more complete liberty than individuals or groups enjoy either to express and propagate their views, or to act as they please within the limits of the law, limits which, except as regards the sale of intoxicants, are drawn as widely as in Western Europe' (356).

Bryce observed that public opinion in America coalesced and was expressed through the usual and predictable means of political parties and newspapers, but that the active associational life of the United States was another important channel for the diffusion and expression of opinion. 'Where the object is to promote some particular cause, associations are formed and federated to one another, funds are collected, the press is set to work, lectures are delivered' (336). Were he writing today, Bryce would doubtless mention Internet-based communities and orchestrated media happenings as tools used by groups to galvanize and influence public opinion. But his essential point would remain the same. 'In no country has any sentiment which touches a number of persons so many ways of making itself felt' (336).

This brings us back to Robert Putnam's argument, mentioned in the previous chapter, about the decline in the importance of associations in America and the resulting decrease in civic consciousness and community. Whether or not Putnam is correct, the point is that Bryce, like Tocqueville before him, was struck by the sheer number, range, and influence of voluntary associations in the United States and was convinced that they were an important part of what made American politics democratic.

The notion of grassroots democracy or, as Almond and Verba put it, the civic culture can be found in the writings of both of these foreign observers of the American scene.

2. ASPECTS OF THE AMERICAN POLITICAL CULTURE

Writers of Bryce's generation tended to discuss political culture in a way that contemporary social scientists find disconcerting. The concept of national character was widely accepted and often not very systematically analyzed. Bryce recognizes the difficulties in generalizing about national character—in this he is somewhat more careful than Tocqueville—acknowledging that there are variations according to region, race, and social class, as well as differences between those who have recently arrived in the United States and those whose roots in America run deeper. In discussing the political culture of America he attempts to describe those traits he believes 'belong to the nation as a whole', or at least the native-born American segment of it. These traits include the following:

- good-natured
- hopeful
- faith in their system of government
- educated
- moral and respectful of the law
- religious
- independent-minded
- busy and restless (with their private affairs)
- inclined to commercial and practical affairs
- mobile
- disposed to work together in associations
- open to change
- conservative (in their fundamental beliefs, institutions, and customs).

Several of these warrant some elaboration.

In describing Americans as *hopeful*, Bryce meant that they exhibited a youthful optimism about their future and the destiny of their country. This has been remarked on by many over the years and is certainly true. One finds this optimism about the future, indeed the idea that America is the land of the future, in everything from presidential addresses since Washington's time to the unreflective confidence that most Americans have that the future is a flight of stairs running upward. This optimism has experienced occasional setbacks, as occurred during the Great Depression, the Vietnam War, and the economic recession of 1990–2 (in the 1992 presidential election, independent presidential candidate Ross Perot was able to make much of the idea that more and more Americans were doubtful that their children would have a standard of living as high as their own). Moreover, there have always been dissenters from the optimistic orthodoxy. Intellectuals, in particular, have often been gloomier about their country's future than is the general public. But on the whole, the optimistic note has drowned out whatever minor choruses of dissent have existed.

Bill Clinton's 1996 presidential campaign provided a classic illustration of how the optimism and future-orientation of Americans can be mined for popular support. This was the candidate whose 1992 campaign slogan was 'Don't stop thinking about tomorrow', words taken from a song by the rock band Fleetwood Mac. His 1996 campaign theme was 'Building bridges to tomorrow', a message constructed around the promise of reaching new and higher levels of achievement in America. His opponent, Republican Bob Dole, seemed to have forgotten that Americans are fundamentally an optimistic, forward-looking people, because his message of recapturing values and achievements that, he argued, had existed in the past was easily turned against him as overly negative and backward-looking. It is fine to venerate and mythologize the past in American politics, but it must be done in a way that connects this past to the future and taps the fundamental optimism of Americans.

Bryce described Americans as conservative, which on the face of it appears to be at odds with the notion that they are optimistic, forward-looking, and believers in 'progress'. In fact, however, there is no contradiction. Bryce acknowledges that Americans are quicker than others to adopt new technologies, to allow market forces to bring about change, and to try novel policies. But, he maintains, 'They are conservative in their fundamental beliefs, in the structure of their governments, in their social and domestic usages. They are like a tree whose pendulous shoots quiver and rustle with the lightest breeze, while its roots enfold the rock with a grasp which storms cannot loosen' (313).

This claim may appear to be untenable in an America that has undergone the radical ferment of the 1960s, the disillusionment generated by Vietnam and the Watergate scandal, and the undeniable changes that have taken place in American society, particularly over the last two generations.

It is, however, still an accurate characterization of the American political culture. At the same time as Americans are forward-looking and unconscious believers in 'progress', they are as attached to symbols, institutions, and norms rooted in their national past as any other people. No President delivers an inaugural or State of the Union address without references to his predecessors (particularly Washington, Jefferson, Lincoln, and, if he is a Democrat, Franklin Delano Roosevelt). The Declaration of Independence and the United States Constitution are, in America, the political equivalents of the stone tablets brought down from Mount Sinai. The essential truth and goodness of these historic distillations of American political values and institutions are widely accepted, even though the meaning of particular values (like equality) and the appropriate operation of certain institutions (like the Electoral College, after the contested 2000 presidential election) may be debated. In this connection it is important to remember that the United States has the oldest constitution of any current democracy and, despite the amendments made to it and the changes in its interpretation over the years, it is recognizably the same document it was in 1789.

Bryce's explanation for the conservatism of Americans is only partly satisfactory. He attributes it to a 'love for what is old and established [that] is in their English blood' (313) and adds that 'prosperity helps to make them conservative' (313). In suggesting that a love for the old and established was in their blood, Bryce was not expressing some biological view of national character. By 'blood' he clearly meant culture, so that the values and traditions that Americans learned, and not their DNA, were responsible for this putative conservatism. Even if Bryce was correct in attributing this conservatism to social learning within a predominantly Anglo-Saxon culture, the long-term problem with this explanation is that the ethnic demography of America has changed dramatically over the last century, making it less probable that the conservative 'instincts' of one group—even if it happens to be the most powerful group politically, socially, and economically—can continue to set the tone for the rest of society.

The second part of Bryce's explanation, however, is more durable. The overall prosperity of Americans has always inclined them to a general acceptance of the status quo and dampened whatever appeal proposals for radical political change might have in a society in which economic hardship was greater and opportunities for material improvement fewer. What many have described as the pragmatic or centrist character of American politics has been due largely to the prosperity that Bryce saw as the best guarantee of conservatism in politics. It is revealing that on the one major occasion when this prosperity was seriously interrupted during the twentieth century, the Great Depression of the 1930s, conservatism was shaken in the United States. The New Deal politics of FDR repositioned the center in American politics, moving it to the left and undermining what might otherwise have been more effective radical challenges to the fundamental institutions and values of the American political system.

Bryce also described Americans as a *mobile* people (he actually used the term 'unsettled'), observing that '[i]n no State of the Union is the bulk of the population so fixed in its residence as everywhere in Europe' (311). He felt that this was, potentially, a serious obstacle to the development of communal sentiments in the United States, threatening to allow for the sort of corrosive individualism that Tocqueville argued was a latent danger in America. But if the mobility of Americans was a factor impeding the development of a sense of being 'rooted to the soil', as Bryce put it, the bonds of community were established nonetheless because of what he called the associative and sympathic character of Americans. Their neighbors may change with a rapidity that would be disconcerting to Europeans, said Bryce, but the openness and widespread aptitude for cooperation and organization of Americans ensured that a sense of community and civic engagement was maintained.

The United States remains the society of territorial mobility, par excellence. One of the possible consequences of this, which Bryce did not mention, is that mobility may contribute to the development of national identities in politics that override regional and local identities. Of course, other factors have contributed to the strong sense of national identification that exists in American politics, including the national media and a party system that is dominated by the same two parties at the national level and in all of the states. But it is also probable that territorial mobility, which has long been and continues to be characteristic of American society, has contributed to the nationalization of American politics.

Bryce's characterization of Americans as an educated people will strike many contemporary readers as no longer apt. Indeed, the state of education in their country has been one of the chief worries of Americans for years, aware as they are of how poorly their students perform in cross-national comparisons of test scores in mathematics and science, how stubbornly high their high school dropout rate remains, and how prevalent functional illiteracy seems to be, particularly among certain minority groups. Bryce believed, as did Thomas Jefferson and Alexis de Tocqueville, that education was one of the pillars on which mass democracy rested. He would have concurred with Jefferson's assertion that 'by far the most important [legislation in the United States] is that for the diffusion of knowledge among the people. No other sure formulation can be devised, for the preservation of freedom and happiness'.[1] And like Jefferson, Bryce believed that most Americans were better educated to carry out their functions as active and responsible citizens than were their Old World counterparts.

The facts of widespread literacy and instruction in the basics of their history and system of government were, for both Tocqueville and Bryce, characteristics of American society that integrated citizens into the political system and prevented the emergence of a class of citizens who were disenfranchised by ignorance and rendered apathetic and mistrustful by a failure to understand and feel part of the democratic system. (Of course, African Americans and women did not have voting rights when Tocqueville visited America, nor was public education available to the members of these groups to the same degree as it was for white males. These inequalities were far from being eradicated when Bryce visited. Nonetheless, universal suffrage for white males and public education came earlier in America than in Europe, a fact that impressed both Tocqueville and Bryce.) The rise of a poorly educated stratum of the population would have been seen by Bryce as a serious threat to American democracy. Contemporary critics argue that this is precisely what has happened in America. Public schools, they charge, too often have failed to perform the democratic functions expected of them. Apathy, cynicism, and ignorance—precisely the opposite of the traits that Jefferson expected schools to instill—are blamed by many, at least in part, on a failure of the public educational system.

It is not clear, however, that the undeniable failure of some schools to serve as more than warehouses for America's least advantaged has imperiled democracy. Mass literacy in America is lower than in some of the world's affluent democracies, and the school dropout rate is higher than in many countries, but these facts need to be viewed alongside the equally striking fact that the participation rate in post-secondary education is, and always has been, one of the highest in the world. Indeed, America, historically, has led the way in mass public education. It is unlikely that Bryce, observing the contemporary scene, would conclude that American schools do a superior job preparing their students for the responsibilities of citizenships, compared to French, British, or Swedish schools. This reflects, however, a catching up and a reorientation of mass education in these Old World societies over the last century, rather than a dangerous failure of public education in America.

3. SOCIAL CLASSES IN AMERICA

The relative absence of class in America was the characteristic, above all others, that struck Tocqueville during his sojourn in the United States. Compared to the Old World where one's class membership was largely decisive in such matters as marriage, occupation, social status, and even legal rights and privileges, and where hierarchically arranged classes were rooted in the feudal histories of these societies, America appeared to be a classless society. It had no feudal past and attempts to create systems of ascriptive right and status inevitably failed. The physical conditions of America and the dominant ethos were unreceptive to European notions of class.

Bryce was also struck by the absence of class in America, or as he put it, the non-European nature of class in the United States. He writes: 'Classes are in America by no means the same thing as in the greater nations of Europe. One must not, for political purposes, divide them as upper and lower, richer and poorer, but rather according to the occupations they respectively follow and the conditions of life that constitute their environment' (314). The meaning that Bryce ascribed to class in America was more akin to what modern social scientists might call 'status' rather than 'class' in the sense that this latter term was used by Tocqueville in contrasting America to Europe. America had classes, Bryce said, but unlike the Old World the outward signs of class membership in America were often difficult to spot and, moreover, American classes were both more open and less antagonistic than classes in Europe.

The classes that Bryce identified as distinct and important in America included farmers, small businesspersons (shopkeepers and small manufacturers), workers, the 'ignorant masses', capitalists, and lawyers. He identifies professionals (physicians, clergymen, journalists) and intellectuals as forming two additional distinctive classes, neither of which he believed had much clout in American politics. Of these classes Bryce believed the capitalists and the lawyers to be the most influential, though he would not have agreed that either posed a danger to democracy (unlike commonplace criticisms of these groups today).

Bryce was impressed by the energy and astuteness of American capitalists, but underwhelmed by their political insight and intellect in matters other than business. Indeed, he clearly found it regrettable that what he called 'the best executive ability of the country' appeared to be so little devoted to public service and generally uninterested in politics except insofar as matters directly affecting their business interests were concerned. Bryce recognized that the wealthy had many means, aside from holding party and public office, to influence politics. The ownership of newspapers was one of these means. But the status that 'titans of industry' had in a land where most people were, as Bryce put it, 'unconscious philosophers' of *laissez-faire* (404), was alone sufficient to guarantee them an influence in public affairs. 'A word from several of the great financiers', he observes, 'would go a long way with leading statesmen' (321).

Lawyers, Bryce noted, constituted the class most active in American political life. 'From their ranks comes a large part, probably a half, and apparently the better half, of the professional politicians' (322). The legal profession furnished most of the great statesmen of the Republic's first century and deserved, Bryce argued, to be called America's leading class. Although they were politically powerful, Bryce believed that lawyers posed no particular danger to the country because 'it is only on a very few professional questions that they act together as a class' (323). On the great issues of the day—trade and tariffs, the regulation of business, public service reform, labour laws, etc.—they were divided and so did not constitute the sort of dangerous faction that Madison had warned about in *Federalist #10*.

The working class in America could, Bryce believed, scarcely be described as a class in terms of distinctive interests and opinions. 'For political purposes,' he writes, 'and setting apart what are specifically called labour questions, there is really little difference between them and other classes. Their [intelligence and education] are as good as those of farmers or traders, their modes of thinking similar' (319). There was simply no way for those who would wish to stir up class sentiment among workers and hostility toward capitalists to radicalize workers who 'feel themselves to have a stake in the country' (317). Their material circumstances were, on the whole, superior to those of their European counterparts and 'the passage from the one class to the other is easy and frequent', factors that undermined whatever sense of class solidarity might otherwise have taken root. What support existed for socialistic and communistic ideas was, Bryce noted, contained chiefly within certain immigrant groups, including recent arrivals from Germany, Poland, and Central Europe.

Below the working class, however, there existed in the great cities of America a sort of *lumpenproletariat* or what Bryce rather graphically labeled the 'ignorant masses' or 'residuum' (319). This class consisted largely of unassimilated immigrants and was, Bryce estimated, not more than about 3–4 per cent of the population (about 2 million was the figure he suggested). (As an aside, it may be worth noting that the size of the so-called underclass in contemporary America is usually estimated to be about 3–4 per cent of the population, depending on how this category of the population is defined. It may appear, therefore, that the unassimilated immigrants that worried Bryce over a century ago have been replaced by a homegrown marginalized group whose existence is certainly a reproach to the ideals associated with America, but which poses no greater threat to American democracy than the 'ignorant masses' that Bryce observed.) Though they were only a small portion of the electorate, Bryce believed them to be easily manipulated and vulnerable to the appeals of dema-gogues. 'Being comparatively ignorant [this class] is not moved by the ordinary intellectual and moral influences, but "goes solid" as its leaders direct it' (320). Bryce regretted the existence of such an element in poli-tics, but certainly did not feel that American democracy was at risk by it. His countryman H.G. Wells, commenting on this class a generation later, was not as sanguine.[2]

Class existed in the United States, Bryce concluded, but it was a quite different and much less politically explosive phenomenon than in Europe. Class solidarity and antagonism were almost absent from the political scene. Although lawyers set the tone for politics and formed the chief pool from which public office-holders were drawn, there was no governing class in America as there was in European societies, nor was there 'one class or set of men whose special function it is to form and lead opinion' (324). Party lines did not coincide with class issues in America, or at least only in a very imperfect way.

Bryce's last observations on class in America make very clear his belief that the absence of European-style class divisions and class politics was one of the blessings of American democracy:

> The nation is not an aggregate of classes. They exist within it, but they do not make it up. You are not struck by their political significance as you would be in any European country. The people is one people, although it occupies a wider territory than any other nation, and is composed of elements from many quarters.

Even education makes less difference between various sections of the community than might be expected. One finds among the better instructed many of those prejudices and fallacies to which the European middle classes are supposed peculiarly liable. Among the less instructed of the native Americans, on the other hand, there is a comprehension of public affairs, a shrewdness of judgment and a generally diffused interest in national welfare, exceeding that of the humbler classes in Europe.

This is the strong point of the nation. This is what gives buoyancy to the vessel of the state, enabling her to carry with apparent ease the dead weight of ignorance which European emigration continues to throw upon her decks. (325)

Later in *The American Commonwealth* Bryce speaks of what he calls the 'pleasantness of American life' (557–64), and he contrasts the comparative hardship and insecurity of the average person's life in such countries as England, Scotland, France, Germany, and Belgium—to say nothing of the misery of Russia's millions of peasants—to the comfort and material well-being that characterize the lives of most Americans. Too many Europeans, not to mention Americans visiting Europe, commented on this difference for it to be considered false or only minor. Indeed, Bryce becomes quite rhapsodic on the subject, putting one in mind of J. Hector St John de Crèvecoeur's famous account of why life in America was preferable for common people to that in the Old World. Bryce writes:

The wretchedness of Europe lies far behind; the weight of its problems seems lifted from the mind. As a man suffering from depression feels the clouds roll away from his spirit when he meets a friend whose good humour and energy present the better side of things and point the way through difficulties, so the sanguine temper of the Americans, and the sight of the ardour with which they pursue their aims, stimulates a European, and makes him think the world a better place than it had seemed amid the entanglements and sufferings of his own hemisphere. (559)

Such observations led Bryce to a discussion of social equality in America. Here he shows his liberal sympathies, arguing not for greater equality of condition between persons, but for greater equality of respect. Servility on the part of those from society's lesser ranks, and arrogance on the part of those higher on the social ladder, Bryce found repugnant. He sounds very much like J.S. Mill when he argues that equality 'raises the humbler classes without lowering the upper; indeed, it improves the upper no less than the lower by expunging the latent insolence which deforms the manners of so many of the European rich or great' (560). In addition, Bryce argues, social equality nurtures national solidarity, 'cutting away the ground for all sorts of jealousies and grudges which distract people, so long as the social pretensions of past centuries linger on to be resisted and resented' (560).

The social equality that Bryce observed in America was, he argued, the product of a society that had no feudal past to bury, no ancient structures of hierarchy and privilege to overcome. He would have approved the sentiment expressed by the German poet Goethe:

> America, you are luckier
> Than this old continent of ours;
> . . .
> You do not suffer
> In hours of intensity
> From futile memories
> And pointless battles.

There was, however, a fly in the ointment of this egalitarian society. It was what Bryce described as the uniformity of American life, an aspect of America that, like Tocqueville before him, he found disagreeable. He perceived more similarity in the opinions, manners, customs, institutions, and even architecture of Americans than in the Old World. While Tocqueville was inclined to attribute such uniformity to democracy, Bryce argued that its sources were to be found in the relative equality of material conditions and, above all, in the newness of the country. Bryce expressed the view that, in time, the monotony of American life might recede 'as the pressure of effort towards material success is relaxed' and as the 'dominance of what may be called the business mind decline[s]' (575). He believed that while the exterior life of America would probably become increasingly uniform (but could he have imagined the same fast-food strips leading into every city; the same chain stores at cookie-cutter suburban malls; the same designer labels, pop culture . . . ?), the interior life of Americans—the life of the mind—would eventually become richer and divergent.

CONCLUSION

Whereas Tocqueville might be described as the first and perhaps greatest philosopher of America, who attempted to discern the meaning for world history of the society taking shape in the United States, Bryce was the first non-American to explain America to the Old World with the clear mind of the social scientist. By this I do not mean that Bryce did not bring passion to his study of America, nor that he did not occasionally allow himself to pass judgment on his subject. This he most certainly did, finding the greater social equality that characterized American society, the far greater influence of public opinion in American politics than in the Old World, and the vibrant associational life of America to be among the superior features of America.

Judgment and speculation of the meaning of America for mankind were secondary, however, to Bryce's primary endeavor. He sought to describe and explain American politics and society for non-Americans, avoiding the ill-informed conclusions, unfounded generalizations, and ideologically motivated assessments that he believed were too characteristic of European commentary on America. The end product of his labors was a majesterial work of enormous sweep and clear-sighted observation. He described the warts, where he found them, but on the whole it was the beauty of his subject that most impressed Bryce. 'America marks the highest level, not only of material well being, but of intelligence and happiness, which the race has yet attained . . . [T]his will be the judgement of those who look not at the favoured few for whose benefit the world seems hitherto to have framed its institutions, but at the whole body of the people' (612). High praise from one of the great students of Western civilization.

Excerpts From James Bryce, *The American Commonwealth*

How Public Opinion Rules in America

Of all the experiments which America has made, this is that which best deserves study, for her solution of the problem differs from all previous solutions, and she has shown more boldness in trusting public opinion, in recognizing and giving effect to it, than has yet been shown elsewhere. Towering over Presidents and State governors, over Congress and State legislatures, over conventions and the vast machinery of party, public opinion stands out, in the United States, as the great source of power, the master of servants who tremble before it. (296)

In the United States public opinion is the opinion of the whole nation, with little distinction of social classes. The politicians, including the members of Congress and of State legislatures, are, perhaps not (as Americans sometimes insinuate) below, yet certainly not above the average level of their constituents. They find no difficulty in keeping touch with outside opinion. Washington or Albany may corrupt them, but not in the way of modifying their political ideas. They do not aspire to the function of forming opinion. They are like the Eastern slave who says 'I hear and obey.' Nor is there any one class or set of men, or any one 'social layer,' which more than another originates ideas and builds up political doctrine for the mass. The opinion of the nation is the resultant of the views, not of a number of classes, but of a multitude of individuals, diverse, no doubt, from one another, but, for the purposes of politics far less diverse than if they were members of groups defined by social rank or by property.

The consequences are noteworthy. One is, that statesmen cannot, as in Europe, declare any sentiment which they find telling on their friends or their opponents in politics to be confined to the rich, or to those occupied with government, and to be opposed to the general sentiment of the people. In America you cannot appeal from the classes to the masses. What the employer thinks, his workmen think. What the wholesale merchant feels, the retail storekeeper feels, and the poorer customers feel. Divisions of opinion are vertical and not horizontal. Obviously this makes opinion more easily ascertained, while increasing its force as a governing power, and gives the people, that is to say, all classes in the community, a clearer and stronger consciousness of being the rulers of their country than European peoples have. Every man knows that he is himself a part of the government, bound by duty as well as by self-interest to devote part of his time and thoughts to it. He may neglect this duty, but he admits it to be a duty. (301–2)

CLASSES AS INFLUENCING OPINION

Classes are in America by no means the same thing as in the greater nations of Europe. One must not, for political purposes, divide them as upper and lower, richer and poorer, but rather according to the occupations they respectively follow and the conditions of life that constitute their environment. Their specific characters, as a naturalist would say, are less marked even in typical individuals than would be the case in Europe, and are in many individuals scarcely recognizable. Nevertheless, the differences between one class and another are sufficient to produce distinctly traceable influences on the political opinion of the nation, and to colour the opinions, perhaps even to determine the political attitude, of the district where a particular class predominates.

. . . the wealthy have many ways of influencing opinion and the course of events. Some of them own, others find means of inspiring, newspapers. Presidents of great corporations have armies of officials under their orders, who cannot indeed be intimidated, for public opinion would resent that, yet may be suffered to know what their superior thinks and expects. Cities, districts or counties, even States or Territories, have much to hope or fear from the management of a railway, and good reason to conciliate its president. Moreover, as the finance of the country is in the hands of these men and every trader is affected by financial changes, as they control enormous joint-stock enterprises whose shares are held and speculated in by hosts of private persons of all ranks, their policy and utterances are watched with anxious curiosity, and the line they take determines the conduct of thousands not directly connected with them. A word from several of the great financiers would go a long way with leading statesmen. They are for the most part a steadying influence in politics, being opposed to sudden changes which might disturb the money market or depress trade, and especially opposed to complications with foreign States. They are therefore par excellence the peace party in America, for though some might like to fish in troubled waters, the majority would have far more to lose than to gain. (321)

. . . the lawyers best deserve to be called the leading class, less powerful in proportion to their numbers than the capitalists, but more powerful as a whole, since more numerous and more locally active. Of course it is only on a very few professional questions that they act together as a class. Their function is to educate opinion from the technical side, and to put things in a telling way before the people. Whether the individual lawyer is or is not a better citizen than his neighbours, he is likely to be a shrewder one, knowing more about government and public business than most of them do, and able at least to perceive the mischiefs of bad legislation, which farmers or shopkeepers may faintly realize. Thus on the whole the influence of the profession makes for good, and though it is often the instrument by which harm is wrought, it is more often the means of revealing and defeating the tricks of politicians, and of keeping the wholesome principles of the Constitution before the eyes of the nation. Its action in political life may be compared with its function in judicial proceedings. Advocacy is at the service of the just and the unjust equally, and sometimes makes the worse appear the better cause, yet experience shows that the sifting of evidence and the arguing of points of law tend on the whole to make justice prevail. (322–3)

ABSENCE OF CLASS CONFLICT

There is in the United States no such general opposition as in Europe of upper and lower classes, richer and poorer classes. There is no such jealousy or hostility as one finds in France between bourgeoisie and the operatives. In many places class distinctions do exist for the purposes of social intercourse. But it is only in the larger cities that the line is sharply drawn between those who call themselves gentlemen and those others to whom, in talk among themselves, the former set would refuse this epithet.

There is no one class or set of men whose special function it is to form and lead opinion. The politicians certainly do not. Public opinion leads them.

Still less is there any governing class. The class whence most officeholders come corresponds, as respects education and refinement, to what would be called the lower middle or 'middle-middle' class in Europe.

IMPORTANCE OF CIVIC ASSOCIATIONS

. . . defects which may be noted in the constitutional mechanism for enabling public opinion to rule promptly and smoothly, are, in a measure, covered by the expertness of Americans in using all kinds of voluntary and private agencies for the diffusion and expression of opinion. Where the object is to promote some particular cause, associations are formed and federated to one another, funds are collected, the press is set to work, lectures are delivered. When the law can profitably be invoked (which is often the case in a country governed by constitutions standing above the legislature), counsel are retained and suits instituted, all with the celerity and skill which long practice in such work has given. If the cause has a moral bearing, efforts are made to enlist the religious or semi-religious magazines, and the ministers of religion. Deputations proceed to Washington or to the State capital, and lay siege to individual legislators. Sometimes a distinct set of women's societies is created, whose action on and through women is all the more powerful because the deference shown to the so-called weaker sex enables them to do what would be resented in men. Not long ago, I think in Iowa, when a temperance ticket was being run at the elections, parties of ladies gathered in front of the polling booths and sang hymns all day while the citizens voted. Every one remembers what was called the 'Women's Whisky War' some ten years back, when, in several western States, bands of women entered the drinking saloons and, by entreaties and reproaches, drove out the customers. In no country has any sentiment which touches a number of persons so many ways of making itself felt; though, to be sure, when the first and chief effort of every group is to convince the world that it is strong, and growing daily stronger, great is the difficulty of determining whether those who are vocal are really numerous or only noisy. (336–7)

THE UNCONSCIOUS BEDROCK OF AMERICAN POLITICAL CULTURE

The term 'ground-ideas' does not happily describe the doctrines that prevail in the United States, for the people are not prone to form or state their notions in a philosophic way. There are, however, certain dogmas or maxims which are in so far fundamental that they have told widely on political thought, and that one usually strikes upon them when sinking a shaft, so to speak, into an American mind. Among such dogmas are the following:

- Certain rights of the individual, as, for instance, his right to the enjoyment of what he has earned, to the free expression of opinion, are primordial and sacred.
- All political power springs from the people, and the most completely popular government is best.
- Legislatures, officials, and all other agents of the sovereign people ought to be strictly limited by law, by each other, and by the shortness of the terms of office.
- Where any function can be equally well discharged by a central or by a local body, it ought by preference to be entrusted to the local body, for a centralized administration is more likely to be tyrannical, inefficient, and impure than one which, being on a small scale, is more fully within the knowledge of the citizens and more sensitive to their opinion.
- Two men are wiser than one, one hundred than ninety-nine, thirty millions than twenty-nine millions. Whether they are wiser or not, the will of the larger number must prevail against the will of the smaller. But the majority is not wiser because it is called the Nation, or because it controls the government, but only because it is more numerous. The nation is nothing but so many individuals. The government is nothing but certain representatives and officials, agents who are here to-day and gone to-morrow.
- The less of government the better; that is to say, the fewer occasions for interfering with individual citizens are allowed to officials, and the less time citizens have to spend in looking after their officials, so much the more will the citizens and the community prosper. The functions of government must be kept at their minimum. (397–8)

THE PLEASANTNESS OF AMERICAN LIFE

I have never met a European of the upper or middle classes who did not express astonishment when told that America was a more agreeable place than Europe to live in. 'For working men,' he would answer, 'yes; but for men of education or property, how can a new rough country, where nothing but business is talked and the refinements of life are only just beginning to appear, how can such a country be compared with England, or France, or Italy?'

It is nevertheless true that there are elements in the life of the United States which may well make a European of any class prefer to dwell there rather than in the land of his birth. Let us see what they are.

In the first place there is the general prosperity and material well-being of the mass of the inhabitants. In Europe, if an observer takes his eye off his own class and considers the whole population of any one of the greater countries (for I except Switzerland and parts of Scandinavia and Portugal), he will perceive that by far the greater number lead very laborious lives, and are, if not actually in want of the necessaries of existence, yet liable to fall into want, the agriculturists when nature is harsh, the wage-earners when work is scarce.... Contrast any one of these countries with the United States, where the working classes are as well fed, clothed, and lodged as the lower middle-class in Europe, and the farmers who till their own land (as nearly all do) much better, where a good education is within the reach of the poorest, where the opportunities for getting on in one way or another are so abundant that no one need fear any physical ill but disease or the results of his own intemperance. Pauperism already exists and increases in some of the larger cities, where drink breeds misery, and where recent immigrants, with the shiftlessness of Europe still clinging round them, are huddled together in squalor. But outside these few cities one sees nothing but comfort. In Connecticut and Massachusetts the operatives in many a manufacturing town lead a life far easier, far more brightened by intellectual culture and by amusements, than that of the clerks and shopkeepers of England or France. In cities like Cleveland or Chicago one finds miles on miles of suburb filled with neat wooden houses, each with its tiny garden plot, owned by the shop assistants and handicraftsmen who return on the horse cars in the evening from their work. All over the wide West, from Lake Ontario to the Upper Missouri, one travels past farms of two to three hundred acres, in every one of which there is a spacious farmhouse among orchards and meadows, where the farmer's children grow up strong and hearty on abundant food, the boys full of intelligence and enterprise, ready to push their way on farms of their own or enter business in the nearest town, the girls familiar with the current literature of England as well as of America. The life of the new emigrant in the further West has its privations in the first years, but it is brightened by hope, and has a singular charm of freedom and simplicity. The impression which this comfort and plenty makes is heightened by the brilliance and keenness of the air, by the look of freshness and cleanness which even the cities wear, all of them except the poorest parts of those few I have referred to above. The fog and soot-flakes of an English town, as well as its squalor, are wanting; you are in a new world, and a world which knows the sun. It is impossible not to feel warmed, cheered, invigorated by the sense of such material well-being all around one, impossible not to be infected by the buoyancy and hopefulness of the people.... (557–9)

The second charm of American life is one which some Europeans will smile at. It is social equality. ...

The naturalness of intercourse is a distinct addition to the pleasure of social life. It enlarges the circle of possible friendship, by removing the gêne which in most parts of Europe persons of different ranks feel in exchanging their thoughts on any matters save those of business. It raises the humbler classes without lowering the upper; indeed, it improves the upper no less than the lower by expunging that latent insolence which deforms the manners of so many of the European rich or great.

... It expands the range of a man's sympathies, and makes it easier for him to enter into the sentiments of other classes than his own. It gives a sense of solidarity to the whole nation, cutting away the ground for all sorts of jealousies and grudges which distract people, so long as the social pretensions of past centuries linger on to be resisted and resented by the levelling spirit of a revolutionary age. And I have never heard native Americans speak of any drawbacks corresponding to and qualifying these benefits. (559–60)

Selected Writings on James Bryce and *The American Commonwealth*

Burton C. Bernard, *James Bryce: The American Commonwealth*. St Louis: B.C. Bernard, 1990. This is a rather straightforward account of Bryce's visits to America, leading up to the writing of *The American Commonwealth*, and of the period 1884–8 during which Bryce wrote the manuscript.

Herbert A.L. Fisher, *James Bryce*. New York: Macmillan, 1927. This is the first biography of Bryce.

Edmund S. Ions, *James Bryce and American Democracy, 1870–1922*. London: Melbourne, 1968. An excellent account of Bryce's thoughts about American society and politics.

Richard E. Neustadt, 'The American Commonwealth Revisited: from Lord Bryce's Time to Clinton's', James Bryce Memorial Lecture 1999, Somerville College, Oxford University. The James Bryce Memorial Lecture is delivered annually at Somerville College.

Hugh Tullock, *James Bryce's American Commonwealth: The Anglo-American Background*. Woodbridge, Suffolk: Boydell Press, 1998. Based largely on Bryce's correspondence, this is an excellent account of Bryce's travels in and impressions of America.

Gunnar Myrdal was an idealist and an ardent internationalist whose life was devoted to understanding the causes of inequality and eradicating them. (*The Royal Library, National Library of Sweden, Stockholm.*)

❧

Chapter 4

UNDERSTANDING AMERICA'S GREATEST FAILURE:

Gunnar Myrdal, *An American Dilemma: The Negro Problem and American Democracy* (1944)

It may seem odd that one of the most influential studies of race relations in the United States, and arguably the most exhaustive, was written by a Swede. Gunnar Myrdal (1898–1987) was a young social economist of some international reputation when he was invited by the Carnegie Corporation in 1937 to assume the direction of the largest research project on race ever undertaken. Myrdal had no background in the field of race relations. Indeed, in his preface to *An American Dilemma* he acknowledges that, prior to being invited to take on this project, he 'had given hardly a thought [to this problem]' and that he 'was nearly stripped of all the familiar and conventional moorings of viewpoints and valuations, [and so] had to construct for himself a system of coordinates' (xix). Why would someone with, by his own admission, no background or intellectual authority in the field of race relations be offered the direction of a project that spanned six years, employed about 150 people at various points, produced a huge and extraordinarily detailed tome, and dealt with what was clearly the most difficult of America's problems?

The answer lay in the very intractability of the problem. The trustees of the Carnegie Corporation were aware that any American social scientist, regardless of his intellectual stature, would be open to criticism on the grounds that his race biased his perspective on this most divisive and emotional of issues. They were also aware that someone from a country with a history of imperialism, such as England, France, Germany, or the Netherlands, would face a credibility problem in the eyes of African Americans. At the same time, the sponsors of this project of unprecedented scale wished to assign its direction to someone 'who could approach this problem with a fresh mind' and from a country with 'high intellectual and scholarly standards' (vi). In the end, the Board of the Carnegie

---

All references to *An American Dilemma* in this book are from the original edition (New York: Harper & Brothers, 1944).

Corporation narrowed its search to Switzerland and the Scandinavian countries, finally choosing Gunnar Myrdal, whose experience of the United States was limited to a year he had spent in the north and northeast, including Madison, Wisconsin, Chicago, and New York, as a young scholar a decade before being invited to direct what would become widely regarded as a monumental analysis of race relations in America.

Myrdal was chosen to undertake this enormous study of America's most divisive problem because of the perception that his personal distance from the phenomenon he was studying would enhance his credibility as an independent, unbiased observer. It is, therefore, rather ironic that his very distance from the circumstances of race in America should today be seen by some as a weakness, rather than a strength, of his analysis. Some would argue that he was guilty of appropriating the voice of African Americans; that, as a white European, his ability to empathize with them and express the experience of their oppression in the United States was necessarily impeded. He clearly believed that racial integration and universalist solutions to the problem of racial discrimination were needed to resolve the 'American dilemma'. This approach, however, is rejected today by some intellectuals and political leaders within the African-American community. What was seen by the Carnegie Corporation as the guarantee that Myrdal's analysis and conclusion would be greeted with acceptance by both white and black America is no longer viewed by all, in these postmodern times, as innoculation against charges of racial bias.

The America that Myrdal visited was, in important ways, a society experiencing crisis and uncertainty. He arrived in September of 1938, when the American economy was still experiencing the ravages of the Great Depression and the reconfiguration of American politics, including the role of the federal government, that began with the New Deal reforms of Franklin Delano Roosevelt was not yet consolidated. Confidence in the capitalist system and the ethos of individualism that was its ideological handmaiden had been shaken as never before in the history of the United States. To the degree that Americans' image of their country by this point had incorporated the idea of America's economic pre-eminence in the world and its ability to deliver on the promise of material progress, and that other countries had come to attribute the same meanings to America, the Great Depression was quite a shock. It opened the door, particularly among American intellectuals, to the possibility that collectivist economic and political systems might be preferable to the American model.

In terms of race relations, the United States of Myrdal's visit, 1938–41, was the America of Jim Crow laws and often viciously enforced segregation, particularly in the South. Myrdal had little first-hand acquaintance with this side of American life prior to undertaking the Carnegie project, and the first two months of his research in the United States involved traveling through the southern states. Like Tocqueville and Bryce before him, Myrdal wanted to gather impressions and data through actual observation and conversation, a process he describes this way:

> We traveled by car from Richmond, Virginia, and passed through most of the Southern states. We established contact with a great number of white and Negro leaders in various activities; visited universities, colleges, schools, churches, and various state and community agencies as well as factories and plantations; talked to police officers, teachers, preachers, politicians, journalists, agriculturalists, workers, sharecroppers, and in fact, all sorts of people, colored and white. . . . The experience . . . was necessary. Without it our later studies will have no concrete points at which to be fixed. (ix–x)

But unlike his illustrious European predecessors, Myrdal had at his disposal extensive human and financial resources—a modern social science team—to assist him in the journey from his initial peregrinations through the South to the production of a study that was expected, by both Myrdal and the Carnegie Corporation, to be an exhaustive account of race relations in the United States and also a springboard to solving what Myrdal called 'an American dilemma'.

As a modern social scientist trained in the first half of the twentieth century, Myrdal believed firmly that social scientific inquiry could and should be undertaken with an eye to solving social problems. Like the great English economist, John Maynard Keynes, whose ideas influenced an entire generation of economists, Myrdal believed that the state, with the advice of intellectual technocrats, could steer economic forces so as to benefit society as a whole. What could be done in the realm of economics could be done in other domains, too. Human behavior, so the thinking went, was relatively plastic and could be changed through policies and institutions that altered the environment in which people acquired their beliefs and attitudes and made choices.

Myrdal was not only an optimistic social scientist, he was also a Swede whose native political culture was much less individualistic and much more statist than that of Americans. This combination made him a rather eager social engineer. The opportunities for analyses like the hugely ambitious Carnegie project to make a real difference were, Myrdal believed, great:

> The social sciences in America are equipped to meet the demands of the post-war world. In social engineering they will retain the old American faith in human beings which is all the time becoming fortified by research as the trend continues toward environmentalism in the search for social causation. In a sense, the social engineering of the coming epoch will be nothing but the drawing of practical conclusions from the teaching of social science that 'human nature' is changeable and that human deficiencies and unhappiness are, in large degree, preventable. (1023)

Tocqueville came to America believing that the democratic experiment unfolding there foretold inevitable change in his native France and the rest of the Old World, where hierarchy and aristocracy were inexorably receding before a tide of democratization. Bryce, too, believed that America was the 'Land of the Future', but unlike Tocqueville he was much less interested in prophesying and philosophical speculation than in describing and understanding American democracy. Myrdal represents a very different case from these other two. In a very real sense, he did not choose America, rather, it chose him. His motivation was quite unlike those of Tocqueville and Bryce. His turn of mind was much less philosophical and there is virtually none of the grand speculation on the historical meaning of the American experience for mankind that one finds in the work of his predecessors. The range of his study is far narrower—he was engaged, after all, to fulfill a specific mandate—but the richness of empirical observation that one finds in Myrdal's study of race relations is far superior. Indeed, while the length of *An American Dilemma*—which, with footnotes, runs to roughly 1,500 pages in its original edition—ensures that relatively few people, even among serious students of American politics, will read it from cover to cover, the wealth of detail is virtually unsurpassed among studies of race relations in America. It is the sort of seminal work one can open at virtually any page and be rewarded with careful observation and scholarship of the first rank.

It is, of course, impossible to do justice to such a work in the space of several pages. Nonetheless, a number of Myrdal's conclusions deserve special mention. First among them must be the reason why he entitled his book *An American Dilemma*. Racial discrimination and conflict were not, after all, uniquely American, nor was a history of slavery something restricted to the United States' alone. Why did Myrdal believe that race relations deserved to be called an *American* dilemma?

1. THE AMERICAN CREED

The answer lies in Myrdal's characterization of America's political culture, the dominant elements of which he summarizes in the term 'the American creed'. The term 'creed' connotes beliefs so firmly held and unquestionable that they have the status of articles of faith. In the case of the United States, says Myrdal, virtually all Americans, of all races, subscribe to the same civic creed, the chief elements of which are belief in the equal dignity of all persons, individual freedom, and equality. These tenets are proclaimed in the Declaration of Independence, enshrined in the Constitution, and proclaimed to be self-evidently true by people of all walks of life and status in America.

Every society may be said to have a political culture, but the United States is unique among the world's democracies, argues Myrdal, in that its fundamental political beliefs are so explicitly formulated and so closely associated with the meaning that America has for its own citizens and for others. It is in this sense that the American political culture deserves to be called a creed, he argues. It is a national ethos, really, a sort of nationalism of universalist principles that knits together at the level of ideals a society that is tremendously diverse. Americans of all national origins, classes, regions, [religious] creeds, and colors, have something in common,' he writes, 'a social ethos, a political creed . . . [that] is the cement in the structure of this great and disparate nation' (3).

By itself this was not such an original observation. Juxtaposed to the history of race relations in the United States, however, the American creed acquired a special poignancy. What the creed proclaimed so openly and unequivocally was dramatically at odds with the reality of life for African Americans. And yet even African Americans subscribed to this creed, despite being acutely aware of their subordinate status in America. Myrdal never really gets at the explanation of this striking paradox, although he comes closest when he talks about status distinction among African Americans according to the lightness of their skin and the phenomenon of 'passing' as white. The explanation probably lay in what Malcolm X and others would describe as African Americans' self-hatred, a condition, they argued, that was generated by white society's portrayal of them and that was then internalized by them, and this resulted in African Americans blaming themselves for their inability to achieve what the American creed promised.

In Myrdal's eyes, the civic creed of America represented the moral heights on which all eyes were fixed, but the reality of America's treatment of its African-American minority fell far short of what he agreed was a noble vision. This is probably what he is getting at when he observes that 'The moral latitude is so very wide in America: if there is abnormally much that is very bad, there is also unusually much that is extremely good' (lviii). This theme is frequently heard in the observations of foreigners on American politics and society. It is the theme of extremes, of polarity, of dramatic contrasts. It was set to music by Montreal-born poet, novelist, and singer-songwriter Leonard Cohen, in his 1997 song, 'Democracy'. There he calls America 'the cradle of the best and of the worst' in what is clearly an observation about what Myrdal called the 'moral latitude' of American society.

This is more than just the familiar refrain about the gap between the rich and the poor in America being greater than in other democracies, a reproach that is heard as often from Americans as from foreign critics. Myrdal was making the point that, judged from the standpoint of race relations, American democracy might well be considered a sham and an abject failure. But this, he cautioned, would be a very great mistake. His was what he called a 'frog-perspective' of the American situation, viewed from swamp level as it were. He contrasted this to the bird's-eye view that would be needed to render a full and fair account of the achievements and failings of American democracy. 'Under a broader perspective,' he wrote, 'the Negro is only a corner—although a fairly big one—of American civilization. This corner is one of the least clean in the national household' (lviii–lix). Polite guest that he was, however, he warned that general conclusions about the United States and its civilization ought not to be drawn from his analysis of this dirty corner of the 'national household'.

Coming from societies with histories of feudalism, aristocracy, and inherited class status, and where these sentiments and structures were often still very much alive, European observers of the American scene inevitably contrasted the experience of class in the Old World to that of the United States. Myrdal was no exception. He believed that Americans' faith in the tenets of their civic creed blinded them to the reality of social stratification in their midst. They were, as we might say today, in denial about an important feature of their society. At the same time, however, Myrdal argued that the '"meaning" of social status and of distinctions in social status . . . varies from one culture to another . . . [and] is usually best defined in terms of the ethos in the particular national culture we are studying' (672).

Inequality in wealth, power, and status in America was not perceived as class inequality and an affront to the American creed because the equality demanded by America's national ethos was equality of opportunity, not equality of economic and social rewards (671). 'The class differences denounced by the American Creed are the rigid and closed ones. The Creed demands *free competition* . . . . Social distinctions which hamper free competition are, from the viewpoint of the American Creed, wrong and harmful' (672).

These observations were made a full decade before the Supreme Court's landmark 1954 decision on school desegregation, before America's experience with affirmative action, and before Americans started to engage with each other in a serious manner on the question of how 'free' the competition really is and how 'equal' the opportunities truly are in their society. Myrdal does not use the term 'systemic discrimination'—no one did during his time—but it is clear from his analysis of race relations that he thought that more than individual prejudice and white bigotry needed to be changed if African Americans were to be brought into the American creed.

2. CLASS AND CASTE

Class lines in America, Myrdal believed, 'are blurred and flexible . . . not defined in law or customs' (675). *Caste* lines, however, were an entirely different matter. Caste involves an ascribed social status that is linked to some personal characteristic over which an individual has little or no control, such as race or ethnicity. In the United States the caste line, or *color line*, as it was more commonly called, was a far more powerful barrier to socio-economic mobility and an affront to the American creed than were any class lines apart from race. The color line existed both literally and figuratively. It was a literal line on the floor in some public spaces, such as bus and train stations, and it took the form of racially segregated train cars, race-specific sections of buses, black and white drinking fountains, etc. Figuratively, its power was no less, taking the form of countless understandings about appropriate behavior, aspirations, and roles for black and white Americans and for the relations between the racial communities. Although the color line imposed limits on both communities, these were felt more acutely and were far more restrictive for African Americans. Myrdal writes, 'The Negro . . . is even more aware of the caste line than is the white man. . . . Since the caste line restricts the Negro without providing him with many compensating advantages, he feels it not only surrounding him but also holding him back' (679–80). He then quotes the African-American leader W.E.B. DuBois, who described the situation of 'his people' in America as being behind 'some thick sheet of invisible but horribly tangible plate glass' (680) that prevented them from entering fully and on equal terms into the mainstream of American society.

Myrdal's discussion of class and caste in American society makes clear that no amount of education, accomplishment, intelligence, or drive would enable an African American to fully breach the color line. At one point he refers to membership in the African-American community as being, in effect, a permanent social disability, as compared to the temporary social disability of white immigrant groups, like the Irish, Italians, and Eastern Europeans, whose arrival in America saw them relegated to the lower rungs of the socio-economic ladder (667). The race of a black person in America, he notes, never disappears no matter how distinguished his or her achievements. An African American in politics is always a black politician. An African-American scientist or writer is inevitably viewed as being, in some way, a representative of his or her race, rather than simply a scientist or writer. The color line never is entirely erased in the consciousness of whites or blacks. The saying sometimes heard in Brazil, that 'money makes you white' (whether accurate or not is another matter), was not one that applied to the United States at mid-century.

The relationship between class and caste in America, according to Myrdal, was—and probably still is today to some considerable degree—influenced by a special dynamic that turns on the relationship that a black person has to the white community. Lighter skin color among African Americans was, Myrdal noted, an attribute that, other things being equal, conferred a higher class status on a member of the black caste. How a black person was viewed and received by the white community was also a factor affecting his or her status among other African Americans. As Mydral puts it, 'an individual Negro's relation to white society is of utmost importance for his class status in the Negro community', and 'leadership conferred upon a Negro by whites raises his class status in the Negro community' (727). Embedded in these observations is an insight that would become commonplace in the wake of the 1954 *Brown v. Board of Education* ruling, namely that the social-psychological dimension of race relations represented perhaps the most serious barrier to African Americans achieving full equality in America. As long as their status depended on how white society viewed them, and their own self-image and self-worth were based on the reflection they saw of themselves in the eyes of another racial community to which they could never be fully admitted because of color, African Americans would not be able to achieve the dignity and equal status that the American creed promises. This realization formed the basis of much of Malcolm X's message in the 1960s. It provided inspiration for the Black Power and 'Black is beautiful' phenomena and has been a premise of African-American studies since then.

3. The Need for Social Engineering

Myrdal rejects the idea that the mere passage of time will overcome racial prejudice in America, arguing instead for a 'social engineering' approach. This would, of course, be the approach taken in the United States after the *Brown* decision. '[T]he social engineering of the coming epoch will be nothing but the drawing of practical conclusions from the teaching of social science that "human nature" is changeable and that human deficiencies and unhappiness are, in large degree, preventable' (1023). He was confident that the social sciences in America were up to the challenge of solving the 'American dilemma'.

Myrdal also believed that the desire to bring black America into the American Creed existed, or at least that the cultural obstacles to equality for African Americans were gradually but irresistibly being overcome. The international crisis during which Myrdal wrote—the rise of fascism in Germany and Italy, Communist totalitarianism in Stalin's Soviet Union, and Japanese militarism in the Pacific—lent special urgency, Myrdal believed, to America's resolution of its racial problems. 'Mankind is sick of fear and disbelief,' he wrote, 'of pessimism and cynicism. It needs the youthful optimism of America' (1021).

Myrdal recognized that international leadership in the free world had settled on the shoulders of the United States, notwithstanding the tug of isolationism woven into American history from Washington's time. He believed that the 'American dilemma', the darkest stain on American democracy, could become America's greatest opportunity. 'If America should follow its own deepest convictions,' he wrote, 'its well-being at home would be increased directly. At the same time America's prestige and power abroad would rise immensely. The century-old dream of American patriots, that America should give to the entire world its own freedoms and its own faith, would come true' (1021).

This was a rather new twist in foreigners' expectations for America. It involved moral leadership in the world. This is somewhat different from the idea of America as a promised land that the Pilgrims held, or the land of freedom and opportunity that is as old as the idea of America, or even the harbinger of democratic civilization that Tocqueville and others saw in America. Myrdal holds out the prospect of America becoming an inter-racial brotherhood united under the rubric of the American creed. The promise of America and its greatest contribution to history could be, he believed, the achievement of the New Jerusalem that progressive social scientists of his generation believed possible. Myrdal had faith in the char-acter of the American people. Speaking of the Americans he met, from preachers to gangsters, he claims to have detected a common goodness among them all: 'they are all good people. They want to be rational and just. They all plead to their consciences that they meant well even when things went wrong' (1023).

So why did things continue to go so horribly wrong in regard to race relations in the United States? 'The fault is', says Myrdal, 'that our struc-tures of organizations are too imperfect, each by itself, and badly inte-grated into a social whole' (1023). Fundamentally good and perfectable people trapped in flawed institutions—the social scientist's dream! Such a situation calls for his special knowledge and expertise to point the way toward the achievement of the New Jerusalem and human salvation.

CONCLUSION

When Myrdal arrived in the United States to take on the direction of Carnegie Corporation's massive study of race relations, he had little famil-iarity with and no firm convictions about America's most deeply rooted and explosive social division. What he had, however, was the analytical tool kit of a mid-twentieth century social scientist, an abiding faith in the ability of applied knowledge to reshape society, and cultural baggage that made him favorably disposed toward state-engineered solutions to social problems. But he also brought to the task of understanding race relations in America an ability to understand this issue against the broader sweep of American history and the meaning that America held for Americans and others. As such, Myrdal was a worthy heir to Tocqueville and Bryce.

It is easy to be cynical about Myrdal's faith in the social sciences and the state to resolve what he called an American dilemma. Since the *Brown* decision America has experienced a half-century of state-implemented desegregation, affirmative action, and race-based quotas in numerous forms, education targeted at changing social attitudes, countless studies and recommendations on race relations, and more. It has made a difference—no one can seriously compare the situation of African Americans today to that during the 1950s—but few would argue that the American dilemma analyzed by Myrdal no longer exists. It is not that Myrdal's diagnosis of American race relations was wrong; rather, he clearly underestimated the intractability of the constellation of attitudinal and institutional factors that blocked achievement of the American creed. In this he has not been alone.

Excerpts from Gunner Myrdal, *An American Dilemma: The Negro Problem and American Democracy*

AN AMERICAN DILEMMA

The American Negro problem is a problem in the heart of the American. It is there that the interracial tension has its focus. It is there that the decisive struggle goes on. This is the central viewpoint of this treatise. Though our study includes economic, social, and political race relations, at bottom our problem is the moral dilemma of the American—the conflict between his moral valuations on various levels of consciousness and generality. The 'American Dilemma,' referred to in the title of this book, is the ever-raging conflict between, on the one hand, the valuations preserved on the general plane which we shall call the 'American Creed,' where the American thinks, talks, and acts under the influence of high national and Christian precepts, and, on the other hand, the valuations on specific planes of individual and group living, where personal and local interests; economic, social, and sexual jealousies; considerations of community prestige and conformity; group prejudice against particular persons or types of people; and all sorts of miscellaneous wants, impulses, and habits dominate his outlook. (xlvii)

A WHITE MAN'S PROBLEM

As a matter of fact, in their basic human traits the Negroes are inherently not much different from other people. Neither are, incidentally, the white Americans. But Negroes and whites in the United States live in singular human relations with each other. All the circumstances of life—the 'environmental' conditions in the broadest meaning of that term—diverge more from the 'normal' for the Negroes than for the whites, if only because of the statistical fact that the Negroes are the smaller group. The average Negro must experience many times more of the 'abnormal' inter-racial relations than the average white man in America. The more important fact, however, is that practically all the economic, social, and political power is held by whites. The Negroes do not by far have anything approaching a tenth of the things worth having in America.

It is thus the white majority group that naturally determines the Negro's 'place.' All our attempts to reach scientific explanations of why the Negroes are what they are and why they live as they do have regularly led to determinants on the white side of the race line. In the practical and political struggles of effecting changes, the views and attitudes of the white Americans are likewise strategic. The Negro's entire life, and, consequently, also his opinions on the Negro problem, are, in the main, to be considered as secondary reactions to more primary pressures from the side of the dominant white majority. (li)

THE AMERICAN CREED

It is a commonplace to point out the heterogeneity of the American nation and the swift succession of all sorts of changes in all its component parts and, as it often seems, in every conceivable direction. America is truly a shock to the stranger. The bewildering impression it gives of dissimilarity throughout and of chaotic unrest is indicated by the fact that few outside observers—and, indeed, few native Americans—have been able to avoid the intellectual escape of speaking about America as 'paradoxical.'

Still there is evidently a strong unity in this nation and a basic homogeneity and stability in its valuations. Americans of all national origins, classes, regions, creeds, and colors, have something in common: a social *ethos*, a political creed. It is difficult to avoid the judgement that this 'American Creed' is the cement in the structure of this great and disparate nation.

When the American Creed is once detected, the cacophony becomes a melody. The further observation then becomes apparent: that America, compared to every other country in Western civlization, large or small, has the most *explicitly expressed system* of general ideas in reference to human interrelations. This body of ideals is more widely understood and appreciated than similar ideals are anywhere else. The American Creed is not merely—as in some other countries—the implicit background of the nation's political and judicial order as it functions. To be sure, the political creed of America is not very satisfactorily effectuated in actual social life. But as principles which *ought* to rule, the Creed has been made conscious to everyone in American society.

Sometimes one even gets the impression that there is a relation between the intense apprehension of high and uncompromising ideals and the spotty reality. One feels that it is, perhaps, the difficulty of giving reality to the ethos in this young and still somewhat unorganized nation—that it is the prevalence of 'wrongs' in America, 'wrongs' judged by the high standards of the national Creed—which helps make the ideals stand out so clearly. America is continuously struggling for its soul. These principles of social ethics have been hammered into easily remembered formulas. All means of intellectual communication are utilized to stamp them into everybody's mind. The schools teach them, the churches preach them. The courts pronounce their judicial decisions in their terms. They permeate editorials with a pattern of idealism so ingrained that the writers could scarcely free themselves from it even if they tried. They have fixed a custom of indulging in high-sounding generalities in all written or spoken addresses to the American public, otherwise so splendidly gifted for the matter-of-fact approach to things and problems. Even the stranger, when he has to appear before an American audience, feels this, if he is sensitive at all, and finds himself espousing the national Creed, as this is the only means by which a speaker can obtain human response from the people to whom he talks.

The Negro people in America are no exception to the national pattern. 'It was a revelation to me to hear Negroes sometimes indulge in a glorification of American democracy in the same uncritical way as unsophisticated whites often do,' relates the Dutch observer, Bertram Schrieke. A Negro political scientist, Ralph Bunche, observes:

Every man in the street, white, black, red or yellow, knows that this is 'the land of the free,' the 'land of opportunity,' the 'cradle of liberty,' the 'home of democracy,' that the American flag symbolizes the 'equality of all men' and guarantees to us all 'the protection of life, liberty and property,' freedom of speech, freedom of religion and racial tolerance.

The present writer has made the same observation. The American Negroes know that they are a subordinated group experiencing, more than anybody else in the nation, the consequences of the fact that the Creed is not lived up to in America. Yet their faith in the Creed is not simply a means of pleading their unfulfilled rights. They, like the whites, are under the spell of the great national suggestion. With one part of themselves they actually believe, as do the whites, that the Creed is ruling America.

These ideas of the essential dignity of the individual human being, of the fundamental equality of all men, and of certain inalienable rights to freedom, justice, and a fair opportunity represent to the American people the essential meaning of the nation's early struggle for independence. In the clarity and intellectual boldness of the Enlightenment period these tenets were written into the Declaration of Independence, the Preamble of the Constitution, the Bill of Rights and into the constitutions of the several states. The ideals of the American Creed have thus become the highest law of the land. The Supreme Court pays its reverence to these general principles when it declares what is constitutional and what is not. They have been elaborated upon by all national leaders, thinkers and statesmen. America has had, throughout its history, a continuous discussion of the principles and implications of democracy, a discussion which, in every epoch, measured by any standard, remained high, not only quantitatively but also qualitatively. The flow of learned treatises and popular tracts on the subject has not ebbed, nor is it likely to do so. In all wars . . . the American Creed has been the ideological foundation of national morale. (3–5)

HYPOCRISY OR HONESTY?

The conflict in the American concept of law and order is only one side of the 'moral overstrain' of the nation. America believes in and aspires to something much higher than its plane of actual life. The subordinate position of Negroes is perhaps the most glaring conflict in the American conscience and the greatest unsolved task for American democracy. But it is by no means the only one. Donald Young complains:

> In our more introspective moments, nearly all of us Americans will admit that our government contains imperfections and anachronisms. We who have been born and brought up under the evils of gang rule, graft, political incompetence, inadequate representation, and some of the other weaknesses of democracy, American plan, have developed mental calluses and are no longer sensitive to them.

The *popular* explanation of the disparity in America between ideals and actual behavior is that Americans do not have the slightest intention of living up to the ideals which they talk about and put into their Constitution and laws. Many Americans are accustomed to talk loosely and disparagingly about adherence to the American Creed as 'lip-service' and even 'hypocrisy.' Foreigners are even more prone to make such a characterization.

This explanation is too superficial. To begin with, the true hypocrite sins in secret; he conceals his faults. The American, on the contrary, is strongly and sincerely 'against sin,' even, and not least, his own sins. He investigates his faults, puts them on record, and shouts them from the housetops, adding the most severe recriminations against himself, including the accusation of hypocrisy. If all the world is well informed about the political corruption, organized crime, and faltering system of justice in America, it is primarily not due to its malice but to American publicity about its own imperfections. America's handling of the Negro problem has been criticized most emphatically by white Americans since long before the Revolution, and the criticism has steadily gone on and will not stop until America has completely reformed itself.

Bryce observed: 'They know, and are content that all the world should know, the worst as well as the best of themselves. They have a boundless faith in free inquiry and full discussion. They admit the possibility of any number of temporary errors and delusions.' The present author remembers, from his first visit to this country as an inexperienced social scientist at the end of the twenties, how confused he often felt when Americans in all walks of life were trustingly asking him to tell them what was 'wrong with this country.' It is true that this open-mindedness, particularly against the outside world, may have decreased considerably since then on account of the depression, and that the present War might work in the same direction, though this is not certain; and it is true also that the opposite tendency always had its strong representation in America. But, by and large, America has been and will remain, in all probability, a society which is eager to indulge in self-scrutiny and to welcome criticism. (21–2)

THE COMPREHENSIVE IMPACT OF SYSTEMIC DISCRIMINATION

To the Negro himself, the problem [of his place in America] is all-important. A Negro probably seldom talks to a white man, and still less to a white woman, without consciousness of this problem. Even in a mixed white and Negro group of closest friends in Northern intellectual circles, and probably even in an all Negro group, the Negro problem constantly looms in the background of social intercourse. It steers the jokes and allusions, if it is not one of the dominant topics of conversation. As inescapable overtone in social relations, 'race' is probably just as strong as sex—even in those most emancipated American environments where apparently sex is relatively released and 'race' is suppressed.

The Negro leader, the Negro social scientist, the Negro man of art and letters is disposed to view all social, economic, political, indeed, even esthetic and philosophical issues from the Negro angle. What is more, he is expected to do so. He would seem entirely out of place if he spoke simply as a member of a community, a citizen of America or as a man of the world. In the existing American civilization he can grow to a degree of distinction, but always as a representative of 'his people,' not as an ordinary American or an individual in humanity. He might protest; if he does it for the proper audience and in the proper forms, he is allowed to protest: but he protests as a Negro. He can criticize, but only as a Negro defending Negro interests. That is the social role awarded him, and he cannot step out of it. He is defined as a 'race man' regardless of the role he might wish to choose for himself. He cannot publicly argue about collective bargaining generally in America, the need of a national budgetary reform, monetary schemes for world organization, moral philosophies and esthetic principles.

. . . The same expectancy of their leaders is shared by the Negro people. The Negro leader, sensing that his own people need him and conscious that his racial origin offers him an easy opportunity for a role in life, thus acquires his characteristic direction. Even women in modern times do not have their souls so pressed into one single narrow furrow of human interests by the tyrannic expectancy of society, although the women's lot in this, as in many other respects, offers the nearest analogy. The Negro genius is imprisoned in the Negro problem. There is throughout the entire history of the United States no single example of an exception to this rule important enough to be cited. (27–8)

The broad masses of Negroes are also enclosed in the prison as effectively by the restrictive expectancy of their friends as by the persecutions of their enemies. [As James Weldon Johnson, the African-American author and educator, wrote:]

> The patronizing attitude is really more damning than the competitive struggle. The stone wall of calm assumption of his inferiority is to the Negro a keener hurt and a greater obstacle than the battle which admits an adversary worth fighting against. It is hard to keep ambition alive and to maintain morale when those for whom you have fondness and respect keep thinking and saying that you are only children, that you can never grow up, that you are cast by God in an inferior mould.

The late James Weldon Johnson sums up this situation of the Negro people in the following way:

> And this is the dwarfing, warping, distorting influence which operates upon each and every coloured man in the United States. He is forced to take his outlook on all things, not from the view-point of a citizen, or a man, or even a human being, but from the view-point of a coloured man. It is wonderful to me that the race has progressed so broadly as it has, since most of its thought and all of its activity must run through the narrow neck of this one funnel. (29–30)

INEQUALITY OF JUSTICE

In most Northern communities Negroes are more likely than whites to be arrested under any suspicious circumstances. They are more likely to be accorded discourteous or brutal treatment at the hands of the police than are whites. The rate of killing of Negroes by the police is high in many Northern cities, particularly in Detroit. Negroes have a seriously high criminality record, and the average white policeman is inclined to increase it even more in his imagination. The Negroes are, however, not the only sufferers, even if they, as usual, reap more than their fair share. Complaints about indiscriminate arrests and policy brutality are raised also by other economically disadvantaged and culturally submerged groups in the Northern cities. The attitudes of the police will sometimes be found among the most important items considered in local Negro politics in the North. (527)

The most publicized type of police brutality is the extreme case of Negroes being killed by policemen. This phenomenon is important in itself, but it constitutes only a minor portion of all police brutality, and the information available on Negro killings by the police does not even give a reliable index of the wider phenomenon. More than half of all Negroes killed by whites, in both the North and the South, were killed by police. But white policemen are also a great portion of all whites killed by Negroes. Even if this information on reciprocal killings between Negroes and white policemen does not give adequate indication of the extent of police brutality, it tells something about the policeman's role in interracial relations.

The majority of police killings of Negroes must be deemed unnecessary when measured by a decent standard of policemanship. The victim is often totally innocent. But the white policeman in the Negro community is in danger, as the high casualty figures show, and he feels himself in danger. 'In the mind of the quick-trigger policeman is the fear of the "bad nigger." Sensing the danger of scared policemen, Negroes in turn frequently depend upon the first shot.' The situation is not this bad in every community of the South; many localities of the Upper South and some in the Lower South have advanced to higher standards.

The main reasons why Negroes want to have Negro officers appointed to police departments—besides the ordinary group interest of having more public jobs for themselves—are to have a more understanding, less brutal police supervision in the Negro community, and to have an effective supervision of Negro offenders against other Negroes. The second reason is not unimportant. Everywhere in Southern Negro communities I have met the complaint from law-abiding Negroes that they are left practically without police protection. (542)

When the Negroes commit crimes against whites . . . there is good reason to believe that the sentences are unusually heavy. The South makes the widest application of the death penalty, and Negro criminals come in for much more than their share of executions. Although no conclusive evidence can be adduced, it would seem that Negro criminals serve longer terms for crimes against whites and are pardoned and paroled much less frequently than white criminals in comparable circumstances. (554)

AMERICA'S OPPORTUNITY

America feels itself to be humanity in miniature. When in this crucial time the international leadership passes to America, the great reason for hope is that this country has a national experience of uniting racial and cultural diversities and a national theory, if not a consistent practice, of freedom and equality for all. What America is constantly reaching for is democracy at home and abroad. The main trend in its history is the gradual realization of the American Creed.

In this sense the Negro problem is not only America's greatest failure but also America's incomparably great opportunity for the future. If America should follow its own deepest convictions, its well-being at home would be increased directly. At the same time America's prestige and power abroad would rise immensely. The century-old dream of American patriots, that America should give to the entire world its own freedom and its own faith, would come true. America can demonstrate that justice, equality and cooperation are possible between white and colored people.

In the present phase of history this is what the world needs to believe. Mankind is sick of fear and disbelief, of pessimism and cynicism. It needs the youthful moralistic optimism of America. But empty declarations only deepen cynicism. Deeds are called for. If America in actual practice could show the world a progressive trend by which the Negro became finally integrated into modern democracy, all mankind would be given faith again—it would have reason to believe that peace, progress and order are feasible. And America would have a spiritual power many times stronger than all her financial and military resources—the power of the trust and support of all good people on earth. *America is free to choose whether the Negro shall remain her liability or become her opportunity.* (1021–2)

Permission to reprint sections from Gunnar Myrdal, *An American Dilemma: The Negro Problem and Modern Democracy*, was kindly granted by HarperCollins Publishers Inc.

Selected Writings on Gunnar Myrdal and *An American Dilemma*

James Angresano, *The Political Economy of Gunnar Myrdal: An Institutional Basis for the Transformation Problem.* Cheltenham, UK: Edward Elgar, 1997. The appendix to this book includes two interviews with Gunnar Myrdal, from July 1980 and July 1982. The first interview is particularly interesting, containing Myrdal's reflections on America and *An American Dilemma* almost 40 years after the book's publication.

Kerstin Assarsson-Rizzi and Harald Bohrn, eds, *Gunnar Myrdal: A Bibliography, 1919–1981.* New York: Garland Publishing, 1984. In addition to *An American Dilemma,* Myrdal wrote many shorter pieces on race relations and other aspects of American society. These, as well as addresses and interviews, are cited in this bibliography.

Obie Clayton, Jr, editor, *An American Dilemma Revisited.* New York: Russell Sage Foundation, 1996. This collection of papers, based on a symposium held in 1994, examines the status of African Americans one-half century after the publication of Myrdal's classic study.

Gilles Dostaler and Diane Ethier, eds, *Gunnar Myrdal and His Works.* Montreal: Harvest House, 1992. Unfortunately, there is not much in the way of good biographical work on Myrdal in English. This collection provides some interesting analyses and angles on Myrdal's life and ideas.

Walter A. Jackson, *Gunnar Myrdal and America's Conscience: Social Engineering and Radical Liberalism, 1938–1987*. Chapel Hill: University of North Carolina Press, 1990. Emphasizes the social engineering theme that informs Myrdal's work.

David W. Southern, *Gunnar Myrdal and Black-White Relations: The Use and Abuse of An American Dilemma, 1944–1969*. Baton Rouge: Louisiana State University Press, 1987. This is an interesting account of how *An American Dilemma* was used during the civil rights era.

During his career as a professor in America and England, Harold Laski's students included many who would become important leaders in their countries. (*By David Low, c. 1935.*)

Chapter 5

࿇

AMERICA VIEWED THROUGH A MARXIST LENS:

Harold J. Laski,
The American Democracy (1948)

Harold Laski (1893–1950) lived and taught in the United States, at Harvard, for much of his adult life. In some respects it may seem odd to consider him a foreign observer of the American scene, given that his career straddled the Atlantic. But despite the many years that Laski spent in America, it is fair to say that he always retained a sort of detached perspective that enabled him to take nothing for granted, but rather to be struck by features of the American experience that perhaps only a foreigner would notice or stress. '[W]hen I first began to teach at Harvard thirty years ago, I realized that, as a European, I had entered upon an experience wholly different in character from anything I had known' (ix). Like Lord Bryce before him, Laski was something of an Americanophile, admitting to what he confessed to be a 'deep love of America'. But he also always remained part of an English intellectual tradition that made him sensitive to the points of difference between the Old and New World. He was truly a transatlantic figure whose life, colleagues, and writings bridged the Anglo-American divide.

Tocqueville's famous book is better known and more often required reading for students of American politics. Bryce's magisterial tome has the double distinction of being the first thorough empirical study of American politics and government by a foreigner and the book that broke ranks with the usual rather negative assessments of the American experience that Europeans had tended to write until that point. (Tocqueville was only partly an exception to this rule. While there was much that he admired in America, it is also clear that he had very serious doubts about the direction of democracy that he believed was foreshadowed by the American experience.) Myrdal contributed the most thorough scientific investigation of America's tragic race problem that had ever been written.

All references to *The American Democracy* in this book are from the original edition (New York: Viking Press, 1948).

But it is arguable that Laski's *The American Democracy* is the single most penetrating study of American politics ever written by a foreigner, albeit one who resided in the United States long enough to call it home.

There is a sense in which Laski combined what is best in both Tocqueville and Bryce. Like Tocqueville he wished to understand America and its politics against the broad canvas of human history. Like Bryce, Laski was deeply immersed in the facts of American life. He had read enormously, of course. But like Bryce before him, Laski had also talked to countless people from the high and mighty of the American political world, including Franklin Delano Roosevelt, Oliver Wendell Holmes, and Louis Brandeis, and to 'students, taxi-drivers, railroad conductors, lawyers and doctors, engineers and business men, who have helped me to form the generalizations I have ventured to make' (x). *The American Democracy* is a work of vast erudition and unsurpassed empirical acuity. And like all truly great books, it appeals to different groups of readers, speaking to historians, political scientists, and philosophers.

There is a sense in which Laski's purpose in writing *The American Democracy* was more purely intellectual than the motives of his three illustrious predecessors. Tocqueville sought in the experience of American democracy lessons for his native France. Bryce sought to fill what he believed was a yawning void of ignorance concerning the actual workings of the American political system and the nature of the American political culture. Myrdal was commissioned to study race relations in the United States. Laski wished to 'make intelligible to Europeans, and, above all, to Englishmen, why America arouses [my] deep love' (ix). But *The American Democracy* also represented the culmination of a life devoted to the study of Western politics and history, a life that produced some of the most influential books of Laski's generation. Published two years before his death, *The American Democracy* was, according to Laski, in fact a generation in the making, going back to his arrival in America. He was living in England when the book appeared, but it is clear that a piece of his heart remained in the United States. In words that testify to his passion for what had become his second home, Laski wrote, 'There is so much more in America than any one man can know. There is so much in it, both of beauty and ugliness, of good and evil, that he cannot put into words' (ix).

Laski's monumental interpretation of American democracy was contemporaneous with Myrdal's, but there are important ways in which the social and intellectual context of his analysis was different. It is impossible to read *The American Democracy* without being reminded over and over again that the Great Depression and Laski's conviction that capitalism (including American capitalism) was in crisis shape the direction of Laski's thoughts. It is important to understand that Laski was one of the most prominent left-wing intellectuals of his generation, and that he was both deeply skeptical of capitalism and convinced that the state needed to play a larger role in the economic life of democracies if real freedom and equality were to be preserved. The Great Depression reinforced his conviction that the policies and dominant ideology of America were not up to the challenge of dealing with such problems as the concentration of wealth in fewer and fewer hands and the polarization of society into classes whose material circumstances and interests were increasingly divergent. Laski's ideas would influence a generation of intellectuals and policy-makers, including such leaders as Pierre Trudeau, Canada's Prime Minister, 1968–79 and 1980–4, who was a student of Laski's at Harvard.

During Laski's lifetime he witnessed the class polarization of politics in England, the rise of communism in the Soviet Union, and the emergence of the United States as not only the world's economic powerhouse but the unrivaled leader of the democratic-capitalist world. He did not hesitate to compare America to the other great empires throughout history, arguing that Americanism represented a 'principle of civilization' that resonated far beyond the borders of the United States. Laski's interpretation of the United States sought to weave together these developments in order to understand the meaning of the American experience for all of mankind and human history.

He most definitely did not believe that the United States was somehow exempt from the laws of human history. Laski rejected the idea of American 'exceptionalism' expressed in the writings of historians like Frederick Jackson Turner, which was commonly accepted by opinion leaders in the United States. He believed that America was becoming increasingly 'Europeanized', by which he meant that socio-economic forces in the United States, as in all industrialized democracies, created objective classes whose material interests were often opposed. These interests would inevitably find expression in party and electoral politics, and should be out in the open, notwithstanding that the power of the dominant classes promoted the myth of America as a classless society.

Laski was not the first to deliver this message, and he certainly was not the last. He cites approvingly the work of such figures as Thorstein Veblen, Upton Sinclair, and Charles Beard, all of whom insisted on the centrality of opposed class interests in any interpretation of American politics. C.

Wright Mills, John Kenneth Galbraith, Robert Reich, and Ralph Nader are among those who have been influential in continuing this tradition of class analysis of America, a tradition that is fundamentally at odds with the notion of American exceptionalism.

Time is often unkind to the predictions of even the most astute political observers, and it is arguable that Laski's confidence that class conflict would eventually break through what he called the myth of classlessness in America, transforming American politics into a species more along the lines of what had already emerged in much of Western Europe by mid-century, has turned out to be way off the mark. Indeed, these days it is more common to argue that instead of America becoming Europeanized, as Laski and so many intellectuals of his generation predicted, Europe has become Americanized in the sense that traditional class politics has lost much of its bite as a far more complex social class map has emerged under modern capitalism than the sort anticipated by the intellectual left in Laski's time. The American party system has failed to become polarized on class lines, as demonstrated in recent years by the rush of Democrats and Republicans to the crowded center, captured in the term 'Republicrats'. The transformation of Britain's Labour Party into a liberal-centrist party searching for a 'Third Way' between capitalism and socialism and the blurring of the traditional politics of left versus right in many advanced industrialized democracies suggest that the rest of the world has become more like America, where class has generally had a blunt edge in politics.

At the same time, however, and despite the protests and denials of some conservatives and libertarians in America, American politics is today much more socialized than when Laski wrote. This was something that he argued had to happen if a critical disjunction between the ideology of American politics and the material reality of American society was to be avoided. Social spending by governments in the United States, the regulation of business and private property, and citizens' expectations for government have all moved in the direction that Laski believed was necessary to prevent crisis and deliver real freedom and equality (although were he alive today he would almost certainly lend his sympathies to a Ralph Nader and not to any of the major figures in the Democratic and Republican parties).

1. THE AMERICAN SPIRIT

Like so many outside observers of the American scene, Laski was struck by the distinctive spirit that pervaded American life and set it apart from the Old World. His choice of the word 'spirit' to characterize the ensemble of values and beliefs of Americans is important. 'Spirit' suggests something larger than a mere adumbration of attitudes. The word resonates with a sense of archetypal ideas, unifying themes, perhaps even a cultural code, that express the meaning of the American experience. Laski devotes the second chapter of *The American Democracy* to what he calls 'The Spirit of America', and it is there that he sets forth his central argument, namely, that the noble spirit of America has become increasingly separated from the material reality of a society that honors it more in word than in deed.

The American spirit that Laski describes is, in his words, 'optimistic, friendly, inquisitive, practical-minded. They find it difficult to believe that progress is not inevitable' (39). It is a spirit that respects success, action, hard work, competition, and the self-made man. The idea of the frontier and of vast horizons, life on a large scale, is an integral part of the confident spirit of America. The following are some of Laski's observations on the American spirit:

> ... the successful man is the happy man, and ... the criterion of success is either the utilitarian one of power—most easily measured by wealth and the influence it commands—or the judgement of one's fellows that one has achieved significance. (41)
>
> ... the American has been accustomed to scan a vast horizon, and this has tempted him to equate bigness with grandeur. It has made him a restless person, anxious rather to do than to be. (39)
>
> There is a real sense in which every American belongs to a self-made generation; he is full of the consciousness that he may both begin anew and climb upwards without the fear that he will encounter some barriers laid by history in his road. (40)
>
> Since the American spirit works in an environment that is constantly changing, it lays great stress on the power to innovate and adapt. It has a veneration for the past; there are few countries where the past is so religiously commemorated as in the United States. But this veneration is wholly compatible not only with the right of each generation to experiment with itself, but, more, with the right of each individual to make his own bargain with fate. (43)

> [The American spirit] is certain that a man is likely to be the best judge of his own interests. It is doubtful whether anything done on the citizen's behalf by government is as well done as when the citizen does it on his own behalf for himself. It is indeed suspicious of government, partly because it associates the ruler with tyranny and constraint, and partly because it has a profound regard for freedom, by which it means letting a man go his own way. (43)

Some of this Laski believed was noble and worthy of efforts to achieve. Much of it he believed was pious nonsense and ideological mystification that served the interests of the few at the expense of the many. On the noble side of the ledger, Laski placed the spirit of innovation, action, practical-mindedness, and the egalitarianism of judging others on the basis of achievement and not according to some ascriptive criteria. These features of the American spirit contributed to the greatness of American society and were received like a breath of fresh air when one left the stuffy confines of the Old World, with its clutter of class distinctions and its accumulated burden of history that tended to lock one's imaginary gaze on the past rather than the future. But the negative side of the ledger in America, Laski felt, was serious and too often overlooked.

The frontier mentality of Americans was one of the aspects of the American spirit that Laski believed was both out of sync with the true character of American society and served the interests of the minority of Americans for whom the positive state posed a threat. Laski understood that the frontier survived in America as a powerful cultural metaphor for new challenges (think of John F. Kennedy's description of space as the 'new frontier', or such generally understood phrases as the frontier of science, or learning, or technology). The 'frontier' is a place in the mindscape of Americans where new things are possible. It is linked to notions of change, transformation, and improvement in one's lot. But it is also linked to notions of individualism and self-reliance, and so the concept of the frontier is fundamentally hostile to the state or any form of collective interference with or constraint on personal freedom. The continuing resonance of the idea of the frontier in America, linked as it is to notions of rugged individualism and a conception of freedom as the absence of constraint, thus serves to impede acceptance of the positive state, including the regulation of private property and the redistribution of wealth.

The problem with the American spirit, Laski believed, was that ideas forged in the America of Thomas Jefferson were in many ways ill-suited to the social and economic realities of the twentieth century. Worse, these ideals were too easily twisted to serve the purposes of precisely the sorts of interests that Jefferson would have found repugnant. 'The power of a tradition to endure', Laski wrote, 'depends upon its capacity to . . . evoke hope and exhilaration from the masses. A ruling class is usually safe so long as the system it controls is able to secure this evocation' (33). No President or other prominent American leader during Laski's time would have dreamt of trying to evoke this hope and exhilaration by appealing to working-class solidarity or any other idea suggestive of class divisions in America. It is instructive that populism has always been an inclusive non-class notion in American politics, pitting the common people against elites, but never drawing the political map in terms of mutually opposed class interests and the systemic exploitation of one class by another. The culprits in the populist critique have been bankers, railroads, the 'trusts', Wall Street, eastern plutocrats, and, more recently, intellectual and political elites. But populism, from William Jennings Bryan down to Pat Buchanan and the attempts of major party politicians like Al Gore and George W. Bush in the 2000 presidential campaign to portray themselves as populists, has never defined the political struggle in terms of irreconcilable class interests.

To do so, Laski argued, would be un-American. Americans and their leaders continued to believe in the idea of American exceptionalism, Laski argued, long after the plausibility of this idea had been dispelled. 'It was believed, despite everything, that America was different, that her destiny was special, that her hopes were on a higher plane than those of any other country in the world' (52).

The reality, according to Laski, was that America had become steadily Europeanized in the sense that industrialization and urbanization generated the same social and political divisions in the New World as in the Old. The difference was that in America the ruling class was able to employ the myth of American exceptionalism, and all that this implied, to ward off European-style social and economic reforms and to discredit the idea of the positive state.

While convinced that the politics of class would eventually assert itself in America, Laski nevertheless believed that the American spirit would remain distinctive. Part of that distinctiveness, he saw, involved the remarkable territorial mobility of Americans, a characteristic of American society that has always set it apart from the Old World. Laski captured the quintessentially American quality that none of his predecessors described as well, the importance of the action principle in America: people and things in motion, evolving, becoming, improving, progressing, conquering. The action principle is tightly linked to the idea of the American as pioneer. Every American, says Laski, at some conscious or unconscious level thinks of himself as a pioneer. Of course, he doesn't clear forests, burn stumps, and till virgin soil. His or her pioneer experience is much less literal than this, but no less decisive in its impact on the individual's outlook on life. The pioneer spirit and mindset lived on in the typical American's willingness to change occupations, to move his or her place of residence 3,000 miles, and then move again, to reinvent himself in ways that his European counterpart would find disconcerting at best.

The remarkable geographical mobility of Americans was, Laski realized, an aspect of what he called the pioneer spirit of America, or what might less colorfully be described as an optimistic openness to change. 'It is hardly an exaggeration to suggest', he says, 'that few Americans, as they pass out of the stage of adolescence, feel the definite conviction that they have made their final geographical bargain with fate. They move on to find a better future. They go on to their new homes with zest and some inner sense of a new world to conquer. They like having to try themselves out against strange people and a community with different ways' (487). In Laski's time, no less than today, it was common to find a family's members scattered across the United States and to observe a willingness to move thousands of miles that was much less common in Europe. 'Americans have always been', Laski observes, 'a mobile people' (486).

The pioneer spirit of Americans, an aspect of which was their remarkable territorial mobility, also had a dark side for Laski. This was seen in the migratory workers that Steinbeck wrote about in *The Grapes of Wrath*, whose standard of life Laski said was 'below the peasant level of Europe' (488). They represented a sort of internal refugee community created by the agrarian revolution in America, involving an inexorable tendency toward larger, more capital-intensive farms and thus increasingly concentrated ownership in the farming sector. The pioneer spirit of America celebrates movement, the search for new opportunities, but the reality, Laski argued, was that the mobility of Americans was not always by choice, nor did it always lead to the better life that the American dream promised.

Above all, Laski recognized that at the core of the American spirit lay the twin ideas of opportunity and hope. '[T]he class structure of American society has never had the rigidity of the European,' he writes, 'and this has made individual opportunity greater, and the chance, consequently, that social pressure would not frustrate the fulfillment of the claims of personality' (498). The American dream, Laski argued, included *the power to dream*, to believe that one had potentially within one's grasp some of the prizes that American society had to offer. When in the 1992 presidential campaign Bill Clinton said, 'I still believe in a place called hope,' this was an evocative double entendre that linked his humble origins—he actually came from a town called Hope in Arkansas—to the deeply ingrained American belief in a better tomorrow for any and all Americans. It resonated powerfully with Americans because it tapped into that spiritual vein in American culture that is expressed in the story of Abe Lincoln—from log cabin to the White House—a story that Laski believed to be more myth than accurate social reality in mid-twentieth century America, but which was kept alive by the agents of social learning in America.

Not much has changed since Laski's time. In the autumn of 2000 I sat in on a first-year American Politics course at a major midwestern university, known to be a bastion of American liberalism, where the professor told his students that the Lincoln story was still the story of America, confirmed by the fact that Bill Clinton, from humble beginnings in an obscure and relatively poor state, could become President of the United States. Laski believed that the American educational system played a prominent role in generating and perpetuating what he called the 'immense mythology', which included an unshakeable faith that 'the path from log cabin to White House is direct and universally open, but also . . . that every man has a full opportunity to climb to the apex of the social pyramid' (23).

Although Laski believed that the rags-to-riches and log cabin-to-White House stories were overdone, that there was more mythology and mystification in them than reality, he was far from being a cynic about socioeconomic mobility in America. He noted that 'the political career has been more fully open to ordinary people in the United States than in any other country in the world' (23), and that 'Lawyer, doctor, engineer, university professor, there is a wide highway along which the humblest may pass to the summit of professions such as these' (23–4). But at least as important as the material reality of opportunity, he realized, was its psychological importance in America. The tradition of deference—of employees to employers and of citizens to those who governed them—was comparatively weak in America. The American worker 'is aware of an economic distinction of class between himself and his employer', Laski observed.

'But he does not easily regard that economic distinction as entailing any social consequence; and he may well feel convinced, especially if he is young, that he will in any case transcend the economic distinction in course of time' (24–5). This is a crucial point: the inequalities that exist in the economy are less likely to be invested with social and political meaning by Americans than by others. This continues to be true today. Americans have a much greater tolerance for economic inequalities than do, for example, Swedes or French, largely as a result of their continuing faith that individuals are the architects of their own destiny.

In the realm of public affairs, the psychology of equal opportunity was also, according to Laski, crucial to understanding the difference between the American spirit and that of Europe. Laski argues that the psychological distance that separated ruler from ruled in America was far narrower than existed in Europe. There was no sense in America that the political elite was a sort of exclusive caste from which average people were barred admission, much less that politicians from the President on down, were unapproachable and deserving of deference and unquestioned obedience. Laski noted that presidents, governors, and all lesser public officials expected, and were expected, to appear open and accessible to the people—to be of them, not above them. This is a long and continuing tradition in America, from Andrew Jackson's public open house at the White House to the electronic townhall meetings that connect contemporary presidents to the tradition of openness established by their predecessors. Jimmy Carter's 1977 walk up Pennsylvania Avenue to the White House after his inauguration and the routine visits of presidents to schools, factory floors, major sporting events, etc. are in the tradition of respecting what Tocqueville observed almost two centuries ago: 'The people reign in the American political world as the Deity does in the universe' (58).

2. BUSINESS, LABOR, AND THE STATE

If one were to point to a single feature of the American political scene that Laski believed to be an obstacle to the achievement of real freedom and equality, it would be the dominance of business values in American life. Nowhere else, he argued, was the outlook of business so generally accepted. In no other society, Laski maintained, were business figures so respected and their accomplishments so revered. And in no other democracy were the state and collectivism viewed with such skepticism, precisely because these were seen to be threats to the businessman and his values.

'[I]it is at least doubtful', he wrote, 'whether there is any capitalist democracy in the world where Marx's famous aphorism that "the ruling ideas of an age are the ideas of its ruling class" has become more profoundly true than in the United States' (50).

The truly remarkable thing, Laski argued, was that these ideas faced almost no serious challenge in any part or from any segment of American society. They were embraced as wholeheartedly in New York as in Los Angeles, he noted, and were even shared by organized labor, the poor, and African Americans. Given this consensus, it was unsurprising that 'there has never, as yet, been a time when the character of the American state power has been shaped by a philosophy which the owning class has not been able to define' (51). The authority and prestige of the great titans of American industry and finance—the Astors, Carnegies, Rockefellers, Fords, Morgans, and others—were truly imperial, Laski argued (165).

A large part of the explanation for the unrivaled dominance of business values in America involved what Max Weber famously described as the Protestant work ethic, an ethic that linked outward signs of success to an inward state of grace. Laski acknowledges the importance of this factor, but adds that there is much more to the explanation, including the absence of feudal-hierarchical structures in America, which, in the Old World, meant that the new capitalist elite faced competition from traditional elites whose power and social prestige rested on control of land, title, or religion. Another factor, Laski argued, was the sheer energy and character of the millions of immigrants to America, most of whom had little material stake in the Old World and whose American dream was not only, or even primarily, a search for freedom, but of opportunities to better their lot in life and acquire things that were denied them in the Old World. He also notes that the challenges of 'hewing a civilization out of the wilderness' (166) placed a premium on practical-mindedness and precisely those sorts of values associated with business. Thoreau might wander the woods and philosophize, but there was little doubt that most of his neighbors took him for a bit of a layabout—if a harmless one—when there were trees to be felled, roads to be built, and business to be taken care of.

But while the roots of the dominance of business values and those who embodied them might be clear enough, it was also clear, Laski felt, that the virtually unchallenged role of those values at the center of American life posed a serious threat to the noble ideals expressed in the Declaration of Independence. This threat assumed three main forms.

1. Groups with interests or ideas opposed to those of business faced a serious legitimacy problem in America. '[N]o radical movement has for long endured in the United States except as a thin thread in the total pattern of the whole' (51). To be taken seriously and to avoid charges of being un-American, groups critical of business dominance were forced to bring their demands and political values into conformity with the familiar capitalist-individualistic belief system. This phenomenon has been generally referred to as pragmatism. In the case of organized labor, says Laski, this has involved an approach to politics that 'has assumed the validity of the American tradition and, within this framework, sought so to act that it could secure the greatest material benefits for its members' (215). Labor, he argues, which ought to have been the major site for values and demands that challenged those of the ruling business class, was content in America to behave like a mere pressure group, moreover, one that neither preached nor believed in class conflict.

2. In a society in which the successful business person is seen as the apogee of achievement and his/her values are accepted as simple common sense, there is a danger that the public space may be treated as inferior to the private realm and civic virtue may wither. Bryce had warned of this when he observed that business tended to attract the best and the brightest in America and, as well, that very often the business leader had little understanding of or interest in public affairs and government, beyond those matters that had an immediate effect on business. Laski echoes this fear that the public space will be permitted to stagnate as the best minds and talents are attracted to other prizes. 'American ambition', he writes, 'is concentrated on the business world and those areas, like the law, which are its dependence' (172). Business persons, the leading figures in America, tend to be poorly informed about public affairs and reluctant to involve themselves in the tasks of government, regarding these tasks as 'an injustifiable interference with the real tasks a man should seek to fulfil' (170). The result, Laski explains, is that a separatism has emerged between the business class and the political class in America, and a tendency for those in the business class—those who rule, even if they don't govern, America—to view government and any expansion of its scope with suspicion.

3. The blind faith of Americans in a belief system that reflects and serves primarily the interests of the business class prevents the adaptation of the American state to the circumstances of modern capitalism and the adoption of policies necessary to promote equality and freedom in a

world where these conditions are denied to an increasing number of people precisely because of the business system that is so venerated. The business ethos of America, compounded of tributes to rugged individualism, self-reliance, and the sanctity of private property and profits, was about a century behind the economic reality of the United States, Laski believed. 'Behind [the dominant ideology],' he argued, 'is a philosophy of economics which is as antiquated as it is unmistakable'(167).

The dominance of business values, Laski saw, operated through several reinforcing channels. One of these was the media. Laski's observations on the political biases of the media are almost identical to those made by Noam Chomsky and other contemporary critics. 'The instruments which shape the minds of citizens', he writes, 'are not freely at the disposal of anyone who wishes to operate them ... for the most part, they are controlled by the vested interests which dwarf altogether the individual and leave him helpless' (617). All three of the major mass media of his time—newspapers, cinema, and radio—were branches of Big Business, whose 'object is not the communication of truth, but the making of profit; and the truth it can afford is rarely the whole truth, but so much of it as is compatible with profit-making'(617).

Laski referred to the mass media as the instruments of propaganda in America. Although he believed they generally served the interests of Big Business, he stopped far short of claiming—as Chomsky does today—that their influence on public opinion was decisive. 'It is quite clear', Laski said, 'that there is no real sense in which they can fairly be called instruments of a totalitarian kind' (622). Although the main tendency of the media was conservative and conformist, Laski believed that the privately owned, profit-oriented media were incapable of stifling dissent and preventing the public expression of challenges to the status quo. 'There is something in the psychological climate of America which resists any ultimate regimentation of behaviour or opinion. Something always escapes the net which is thrown about the people' (622–3). Chomsky might disagree, but the considerable media coverage of Ralph Nader's 2000 presidential campaign proved Laski's point.

A second channel through which business values dominated was, according to Laski, the party system. '[I]t is difficult to argue', Laski wrote, 'that a presidential election in America is, with all its excitement, very different from a choice by the voters between two wings of a single Conservative party' (130). The hammerlock of the two major parties on American elections was, he believed, a serious obstacle to the emergence of a left-wing challenge to the status quo. Laski laid part of the blame for this on organized labor, which he characterized as being without a coherent political philosophy and guided by short-term expediency, willing to trade its support to one candidate or another, or one party or another, in order to achieve particular measures. Unlike the experience of Western Europe, where trade unions tended to be crucial in giving birth to socialist parties or at least to be the main pillar of support for such parties, organized labor in America tended to avoid formal alliances with political parties, conceiving of itself as an interest group rather than a social movement with a comprehensive social and political agenda. This, in turn, impeded the development of working-class consciousness and political mobilization, thereby playing into the hands of business interests.

Laski was, however, confident that the situation of one party masquerading as two parties would eventually change and that a socialist party with widespread popular support was bound to emerge in America. He argued that American labor would be driven to take independent political action, creating its own political party along the lines of socialist principles, and that once this happened the similarity of the Republican and Democratic parties and their neglect and even hostility to working people's interests would become increasingly apparent. A scenario similar to that which had already occurred in Britain would transpire: as class consciousness increased, support for the new socialist party—by whatever name it might go—would grow, and one of the historically dominant parties would be squeezed off the map. The United States would repeat the experience of Europe, Laski argued, and he took heart from what he believed was exactly this sort of growing class consciousness and left-right party realignment in Canada, where a socialist party had actually been elected to power in Saskatchewan, one of the Canadian provinces (136–7). This, he believed, was the only hope and salvation for an America truly respectful of equality and freedom. Organized labor's decision to work through the major parties had not been without success, Laski acknowledged. But the economic oligarchy that labor confronted in mid-twentieth-century America was so formidable, and the historically dominant parties' ties to business and its values so tight, that only a 'real radical party, built upon the mass basis of the trade unions' (251), could overcome what he saw as a creeping meanness in American life. The labor unions' task, Laski argued, 'is to create the understanding that the American dream is in danger, and that those who join its ranks are preserving the splendour of the American dream' (263).

It goes without saying that Laski would have been very disappointed by the course of events over the past half-century. Union membership in the United States rose after the World War II, but has plummeted since the 1960s. No labor-socialist party has emerged as a serious threat to the major parties' dominance. Organized labor has intensified its ties to one of these parties, the Democratic Party, but it is merely one voice—albeit an influential one—within the coalition of interests and ideas that is the Democratic Party. Americans are hardly more class-conscious today than two generations ago, and their skepticism about unions—a skepticism kept alive, it might be added, by Hollywood's reinforcement of the corrupt union image seen in a film like *Hoffa*—remains deep.

Education in America, Laski argued, also contributed to the dominance of business values. He observed, as had Tocqueville and Bryce before him, that education at all levels was expected to perform a utilitarian function, harnessed to the acquisition of practical knowledge and skills. 'The Americans are a serious and practical people', he said, and 'to expect a nation which wrested civilization from nature to be interested in education merely for the sake of the play of the mind would be folly' (323). The anti-intellectual streak that has always existed in American culture—the disdain for mere philosophizing and theorizing whose justification is not the creation of an improved widget or a better citizen, the achievement of more wealth, or a cure for some disease—has its roots in the very pragmatic way in which most Americans have viewed education and the proper role of schools.

This pragmatism reaches to the highest levels of the American educational system. Laski thought it revealing that the governing bodies of American universities, their trustees, were typically men judged to be successful by the standards of a civilization dominated by business values. Lawyers, bankers, business persons, and an occasional cleric represented the pool from which trustees tended to be drawn. Their choice of university president is, Laski argued, strongly influenced by business values. In words that have a very contemporary ring, he said, the university president 'must cultivate the foundations, wealthy men, and big corporations. . . . He dare not offend the rich upon whom he depends. He must be interested less in the digestion of experiments than in their extension. Bigger library buildings, larger dormitories, a better stadium, a more spacious chapel . . . are the key to this ideal' (350). The president of a great and prestigious American university is a sort of ambassador between the worlds of learning and business, but must never forget which world pays the bills that ensure the eminence of his institution.

The unsurprising result of these intimate ties to the world of business, Laski argued, was that the professoriate, with relatively few notable exceptions, tended to be rather timid in their teaching and writing, aware that there were few rewards, and, potentially, serious sanctions, for challenging the values and institutions upon which business relied. Laski points to the careers of Charles Beard and Thorstein Veblen, two of the most prominent critical social scientists of their generation, as illustration of the stifling atmosphere that existed within academe (358).

The radicalization of American academe that occurred during the 1960s would probably have heartened Laski, as would the current perception of universities as bastions of liberal-left challenges to business dominance. But while the range of ideological expression in American academe is wider today than in the past—it is hard to imagine Angela Davis, former Black Panther and convicted felon, currently teaching at the University of California, being hired in Laski's time—there is also a widespread perception that business values are more influential, and university dependence on business greater, than at any time in America's history.[1]

Religion, too, Laski argued, reinforced the social dominance of the business class and its values. 'There has never been', he writes, 'that gap between the standard of the Churches and the standard of the secular world which has put the latter on the defensive before its critics' (313). Without denying that particular religions and religious figures have been nodal points for social criticism—Laski mentions, for example, the social gospel movement in the early 1900s (318)—he argues that churches in America have been more important in promoting *religiosity* than *religion*. 'I mean by religiosity the support of the folklore of some specific social order by bringing to its general support the magic aid of an institution which claims its foundation in the will of God' (321). The churches, he claimed, encouraged acquiescence and acceptance of the values of the secular-materialist society in which they were situated, not the questioning or even the overthrow of these values. The political ascendance of the Moral Majority during the 1980s and the continuing influence of faith-based conservatism in American politics would not have surprised Laski.

Buttressed by the churches, the educational system, and the mass media, and without a serious challenge from organized labor, business and its values dominated America to a degree not found in any other society. The politicians governed, Laski conceded, but the business class ruled.

3. Laski's Paradox

> There is an important sense in which the very vastness of the opportunity America offered its citizens was inimical to the fulfillment of what a democratic community implies. (17)

There is a very real sense in which Laski's *The American Democracy* is written in the shadow of Frederick Jackson Turner's great thesis, *The Frontier in American History*, published in 1893. Laski believed Turner to be one of the greatest of American historians, but he also thought that Turner's argument about the decisive impact of the frontier experience on the culture and institutions of American society, including in those parts of the United States that had been settled long before the expansion into the Ohio Valley and west of the Mississippi, and the relative unimportance of European influences on the American political tradition, was vastly exaggerated. 'Turner', he wrote, 'provided the grounds for defending the thesis of a native and independent American culture. . . . He was not merely writing history; he was also justifying the American claim that the United States was, in a special degree, the guardian of democratic civilization' (740–1). Many others had argued that America was exceptional, its destiny guided by stars other than those that ruled the destinies of Old World societies—that the New World had produced, in Jefferson's words, a New Man, unfettered by the repressive habits and history of Europe—but none had provided the sort of historical explanation for this exceptionalism found in Turner's work. In a well-known passage from *The Frontier in American History*, Turner wrote:

> Other nations have been rich and powerful, but the United States has believed that it had an original contribution to make to the history of society by the production of a self-determining, self-restrained, intelligent democracy. It is in the Middle West that society has formed on lines least like Europe. It is here, if anywhere, that American democracy will make a stand against a tendency to adjust to a European type.[2]

Turner was brilliant, Laski believed, but fundamentally wrong. According to Laski, those who argue that the American experience, upon which the ideas associated with the American spirit rest, is unique must come to grips with the historical fact that the disappearance of frontier America changed everything. Turner's frontier thesis of American democracy was, Laski maintained, an attempt to defend and justify the old Jeffersonian ideal of the United States as a republic of freemen, based on values and institutions rooted in the ideal of a democracy of small property-holders. This, Laski argued, had ceased to be relevant to American conditions by the mid-nineteenth century, but continued to exert a romantic influence on the minds of Americans well after it was clear that American society, in terms of industrialization, urbanization, and employer-employee relations, was developing along the same lines as Europe. Jefferson's idea of the American as a New Man, Turner's frontier thesis of American democracy, the idea of American exceptionalism, and the extraordinary faith in individualism that was characteristic of American culture all represented what Laski described as 'an anachronistic deposit from the days when almost all men saw immense horizons open before them' (745).

Karl Marx, not F.J. Turner, got it right, thought Laski. Writing just after the American Civil War, Marx had argued that 'as capitalist advance devoured the independence of the individual American, it would create relations between him, as an industrial employee, and the great corporations upon which he was dependent, which would transcend in their psychological implications all the traditions to which the agrarian community of peasant farmers owning their own land would give rise' (743).

Laski's paradox boils down to this: the open frontier and the unparalleled opportunity that America had offered its citizens provided the basis for a highly individualistic belief system that, far from being consistent with democracy, actually impeded the adoption of reforms necessary to promote real equality and freedom in a society dominated by Big Business and where the ideal of the individual as the author of his own destiny was more romantic myth than sociological reality. America had become Europeanized, in terms of its social and economic relations, but was in denial because of the persistence of an ideal of Americanism that served the interests of the ruling class. This paradox would eventually explode as the facts of modern conditions in America became undeniable and when labor leaders in the United States came to realize that they needed their own political vehicle—a labor-based socialist party—to achieve real reform. The development of class-consciousness in America could not be held up forever.

Conclusion

Laski's belief that class would become the key dividing line in American political life continues to attract followers, particularly among left-wing members of the intelligentsia. In retrospect, however, it is hard to escape the conclusion that he and the generation of left-wing intellectuals among whom he was such a prominent figure were mistaken. Instead of America becoming Europeanized, the experience of the last few decades suggests that Europe may, in some ways, have become Americanized, or at least that the United States has proven to be stubbornly resistent to the sort of historical trajectory that Laski believed inevitable in industrialized democracies.

Laski failed to anticipate three developments that have been responsible for the persistence of the individualistic spirit of America. One is the fact that America has remained a middle-class society. Even though the gap between the top and bottom rungs of the American socio-economic ladder has widened, most people still occupy middle rungs on the ladder. The sort of dramatic polarization in class circumstances that Laski expected to occur and the pauperization of the working class that all left-wing intellectuals since Marx believed inevitable have not happened. Second, government regulation of business, limitations on the rights of private property, and the redistribution of wealth through state spending and taxation have occurred in the United States as elsewhere, although the extent of these developments clearly does not satisfy everyone and has not gone as far as in Canada or some Western European democracies. All this has happened under non-socialistic political parties, the Democratic Party, in particular, proving capable over the years of accommodating the demands of groups advocating social and economic reform.

Finally, Laski did not anticipate the role that the media would play in nurturing the vitality of the frontier mentality and the individualistic ethos, which he expected to recede before the pressures of social and economic change. The imagination of Americans, their symbolic universe or mindscape, is powerfully influenced by the images and stories that television and film provide. On the whole, these media continue to convey an image of America as middle class and individualistic, full of opportunities in its economic and political life, and where the powerful do not always win. The very successful Hollywood film *Erin Brockovich* is one of the more recent examples of the long-standing American morality tale that sees the little person, representing the hopes and interests of the common man, win against powerful vested interests. Of course, if such a story was not based on real-life circumstances, as it was in this case, it would resonate less powerfully. A dominant ideology cannot be too disconnected from social reality and hope to survive unless there is a massive investment in repression to reinforce the false consciousness promoted by an ideological apparatus controlled by the powerful. Some critics maintain that this investment in fact exists, that the prison system and the justice system are instruments for controlling those at the bottom of the class ladder in America. But there is more than a touch of intellectual arrogance and psychological distance from the lives of most Americans in the claim that their image of themselves and their society is the groundless construction of the propaganda machines of the powerful.

In the end, Laski was wrong about the future that awaited America in the second half of the twentieth century. In this he was not alone. Class has failed to become the defining fault line in American politics, organized labor has failed to transform itself into a vehicle for challenging the capitalist system and individualistic ethos of America, and the frontier self-image that Americans have continues to be more powerful than he would have imagined possible. None of this detracts, however, from the monumental stature of his interpretation of a society and its politics that had become a second home to Laski.

༈

Excerpts from Harold J. Laski,
The American Democracy

A NEW CIVILIZATION

Most of the heritage of past civilizations has gone into the making of American democracy. Europe and the Far East have alike nourished its rise and development; it has strains from the African continent which lie deep in its foundations. In the four and a half centuries since it emerged into the historic consciousness, it has passed from the epoch in which it was an object of colonial ambition to the epoch where it stands, independent, at the summit of political power. And in that momentous period there can be no sort of doubt but that its impact has changed the outlook of mankind wherever there has been the power to reflect on the meaning of human affairs. No state, until our own day, has done so much to make the idea of progress a part of the mental make-up of man. No state, either, has done more to make freedom a dream which overcame the claims both of birth and of wealth. It has been, in an impressive way, a refuge for the oppressed, alike in the political and in the religious field, for at least the period since the Pilgrim Fathers landed on the rocky shores of New England. It has offered to the common man an opportunity of self-advancement such as he has never known elsewhere until the Russian Revolution of 1917. Few countries have ever developed material resources on so vast a scale. Few countries have ever been able to move so swiftly from the circumference to the centre in their impact upon civilization. If it has often been hated and even more often envied, there has always been a perception, even in the hatred and the envy, that it occupied a unique position among the nations of the world. Now it stands close to the zenith of its fortunes. For something like the next generation it is difficult to doubt that world politics will be set in the context of American purposes. Upon the use it decides to make of its overwhelming productive power, no small part of the fate of Europe and Asia, perhaps of Africa as well, is bound overwhelmingly to depend. (3)

THE TRADITIONS OF AMERICA

From the very outset the psychological roots of the American idea have been built upon the foundation of expansionism. There was expansion territorially; there was expansion in the power to utilize the vast resources which, until 1929, seemed to have no limit. There was, too, a cultural expansion symbolized, perhaps, above all, in the faith in education and the intensity with which applied science has been accepted as a normal part of living.

The very bigness of America has an importance in the formation of its tradition which it is not easy to overestimate. It creates the belief that America is different, is somehow exceptional, that there is reserved for its citizens another destiny from that which is to befall the Old World. The spaciousness of the United States as a physical entity makes the idea of unlimited horizons, of constant discovery, of novelty that is always imminent, part of the background against which each American is set. However much of the colonial period may be dependent upon European ways of thought, their adaptation to American use always involves some change of greater or lesser profundity. This is, I think, because at the base of the tradition is, even when unconsciously, the thought in every man that he is somehow a pioneer, and, therefore, the growth of a conviction that there is no problem he cannot tackle. If he is an immigrant he is a pioneer because he has made the break with the Old World; if he is the child of an immigrant he is a pioneer because he is affirming in his own person the finality of the break; and if he is an American, like the remarkable Adams family, of long standing, he is a pioneer because he belongs to the small group of men who have shaped the contours of the New World.

This concept of the pioneer penetrates every nook and cranny of the American tradition. It explains why the ordinary American rarely assumes that any career upon which he embarks is, outside such special professions as medicine and the churches, the final career in which he will end. Thomas Jefferson is a polymath who attains distinction in every subject he touches; Benjamin Franklin is only less eminent as a diplomat and statesman than as a scientist . . . or there is Andrew Jackson, farmer, merchant, lawyer, soldier, congressman, and, finally, president of the United States. Towering above all is the majestic figure of Abraham Lincoln, lonely, aloof, tragic, who grows from the illiteracy of a home where there is little but failure and poverty to impose himself not merely on the mind of America, but on the mind of all civilization, as the supreme figure in the democratic tradition of the nineteenth century. As one examines the significance of these men, it is impossible not to conclude that they represent a new category in the conventional distribution of the human beings who search for the means to rule their fellow-citizens.

... [T]here is inherent in the American tradition the spaciousness of hope and the exhilaration that hope conveys; and it is the greatness of this quality that it brings out in so many the zest for adventure, the sense of ambition, the willingness to break the routines in which they have been enclosed. . . .

The American tradition is, in essence, an individualistic tradition which has tended to look upon the State with doubt or suspicion. In part, of course, this attitude stems from the religious background of the seventeenth century; the pioneers were men and women seeking to escape from a persecuting government to which their truths were unacceptable. That does not mean for a moment that the pioneers were generally in favour of toleration. . . . there was the variety of national origin of the settlers themselves, and the impossibility, in its light, of maintaining for long any rigid form of orthodoxy. No doubt the general basis of the American tradition was the Christian heritage from Europe; and no doubt, also, the clergy occupied a specially important place in its making. But it was rarely possible for any of the thirteen colonies to maintain for very long the union of some given Church with the State. And the outcome of this tendency to separation was to emphasize the idea that the individual should find his own pathway to salvation. The release this effected in the sphere of belief had inevitable repercussions far beyond its boundaries.

The first object of the settler on American soil was to be the master of his environment. He had to build his house, to sow his crops; and his wife had to provide the largest part of those needs which could only slowly come to count upon the results of the division of labour. The consequence of this was that few Americans, comparatively, lived by owning merely; and this fact conferred upon the idea of toil a claim to dignity, a sense of self-reliance, which gave the idea of individualism a special sanctity. By the War of Independence about one American in ten lived in a town. This meant that most of them assumed that they must depend upon themselves for the provision of services we now regard as a normal function of the government. And from this it followed that the individual citizen became what he could make himself, so that he tended to think of any restraint placed by authority upon his power to develop his fortunes as in itself a harmful thing. The tradition, therefore, looked upon the government as, above all, an organ of defence and order. And this attitude was even intensified by the colonial experience of restraints imposed upon the economic prospects of American citizens by the restrictive legislation of the mother-country. (5–7)

The other factor of importance is the need to realize that the primitive values of the pioneer, which loom so large in the American tradition, are psychological as well as geographical in character. It is not merely on the frontier that men seize the opportunity before their eyes; they seize it also in that settled realm where, in a new industry or a new method of organization, there is the big chance present for the taking. Capitalist industrialism presented to men like Astor and Vanderbilt, Jay Gould and Rockefeller, exactly the same chance in kind as virgin America presented to the Puritan settlers of the seventeenth century. . . . The central ideal in the perspective of which all values are set is the lure of vast and sudden wealth. Its influence on every aspect of American life is hardly capable of over-estimation. It infects the politician, the lawyer, the priest, even the teacher. And it infects them while they are troubled in their consciences by that American dream of equal opportunity which is always challenging the values of a business civilization. (33)

The power of a tradition to endure depends upon its capacity to command a continuing faith; and this, in its turn, depends upon its power to evoke hope and exhilaration from the masses. A ruling class is usually safe so long as the system it controls is able to secure this evocation. For so long as men have the sense that the road is open, they do not feel that they must take to jungle paths. No student of American history can fail to observe that, the Negro problem alone apart, its mental climate is one of discovery, expansion, optimism. There are periods, no doubt, of crisis; but the vitality of the scene is so abundant that it is rare for men to be unable to overcome them rapidly. The legend of America is of unlimited spaces, of endless opportunities, of resources which know no bounds. (33–4)

THE DAILY MANUFACTURE OF MYTHOLOGY

It is interesting to realize the methods by which this belief [in capitalism] has been maintained. It is interesting because, alongside the political democracy so deeply rooted in the American tradition, most of the instruments through which the picture of the scene to be interpreted to the American is painted have become a branch of Big Business. That is true of the cinema; it is true of the radio, it is true of the overwhelming proportion of the press. Even if, here and there, a source of doubt whether the habits of Big Business fit into the habits of a democratic way of life find means of expression, in some of Mr Chaplin's films, for instance, in the remarkable use to which President Roosevelt put the radio, in a small number of weeklies whose total circulation does not add up to the influence of a single publication like the *Saturday Evening Post*, or in the occasional columns of an eminent though small-town journalist, like the late William Allen White, the incidence of the whole picture is enormously and continuously tilted towards the support of vested interests against the democratic tradition for which America came into being as an independent nation. And the immense influence of advertising moves in the same direction. (21)

And to the immense weight of these influences must be added the power of Big Business in the educational world as well as in the realm of scientific research. The schools, where they are publicly controlled by the state governments, are almost wholly devoted to the exposition of a faith which makes 'getting on in the world' practically an article in a religious creed; and, where they are private institutions, they do not even question the validity of the traditional economic system. In the field of higher education the power of wealth is almost overwhelming. Where the university or college is maintained by the state, it is difficult for radical theory to express itself in any subject which may endanger the rights of property; it is typical that the University of Montana should have dismissed a distinguished professor of economics for proving that, over long years, the great copper companies had evaded their fiscal obligations. The university or college which depends on private endowment is, in some ways, more liberal in outlook than the university or college dependent upon state funds; but in any field of study which raises the issue of property it is rare indeed to find that the challenging mind is sure of a welcome. . . .

The simple fact is that the American educational system reflects the character of the economic system within which it functions. It could hardly, indeed, be otherwise. One could no more expect a capitalist society to permit its teachers generally to undermine the foundations of private property than one could expect the schools and universities of the Soviet Union to admit teachers whose energies are devoted to expounding the fallacies of Marxism, or the authorities in the academic institutions of Vatican City to exhibit an eager tolerance for scholars who think more highly of Strauss and of Bauer, of Loisy and of George Foot Moore, than of the representatives of the official outlook. No society ever permits the foundations of its system to be called into question unless it is certain that it will triumph overwhelmingly in the reply.

What is of interest in the working of the American educational system is less its subordination to the effective sources of sovereignty than the immense mythology it has contributed to the shaping of the American tradition. Few aspects of its life have done so much to persuade the masses not only to believe that the path from log cabin to White House is direct and universally open, but also to accept the faith that every man has a full opportunity to climb to the apex of the social pyramid. (22–3)

RUGGED INDIVIDUALISM AND MISTRUST OF THE STATE

It may be doubted, further, whether any previous community in history has laid so great an emphasis upon the obligations of the individual citizen to hew his way to success. With, of course, exceptions, and even notable exceptions, the faith of American business has been the simple conviction that a man's failure in life is reasonably attributable to his own faults. No democracy has been less interested in its failures; in an economic sense, no democracy has so magnificently rewarded its successful men or been so continuously convinced that prosperity was always round the corner. It is, I think, significant that so deep is this conviction that it has not yet proved possible in the United States to create a permanent working-class party. The average American does not really doubt either that he himself belongs to the middle class, or, at least, that his children will do so. Aware that his standard of life, if he is a white man, is far beyond the standard attained anywhere save in New Zealand, he draws the inference therefrom that the cause of this success lies in the private ownership and control of property. The state power is there to defend the American way of life against aggression, internal or external; and it may be used legitimately to educate the nation's children, to lay down standards of performance in such realms as food and drugs, or railroads, or the cleaning of streets. But most Americans have a sense of deep discomfort when they are asked to support the positive state. They tend to regard it as a method of eroding the responsibilities of the individual. They tend to feel that what is done by a governmental institution is bound to be less well done than if it were undertaken by individuals, whether alone or in the form of private corporations. The main clue to the understanding of American enterprise is the need to realize that articulate America still looks upon the state as the enemy as soon as it moves from the area of defence or of police. Whatever functions it performs additionally to these are in the nature either of a *pis aller*, or, like the Geological Survey or the Bureau of Standards, something it would not pay citizens to undertake as a private enterprise. (166–7)

OPIATE OF THE MASSES

[N]o one who examines with care American religious experience in the first half of the republic's history has the right to suppose that its influence decisively shaped the character of that history. It brought immense consolation to many; it helped to organize many important canons of behaviour; it encouraged, in appropriate areas, a considerable number of social and philanthropic causes. But in a world which seemed committed to the principle of *laissez-faire* no Church was seriously able, and few seriously attempted, to do more than mitigate the major tragedies of *laissez-faire*. The real centre of power rested with the wealthy to whom the Churches were a valuable instrument for making the poor contented with their lot. That, indeed, was seen quite clearly by Horace Greeley. 'To the conservative', he wrote, 'Religion would seem often a part of the subordinate machinery of Police, having for its main object the instilling of proper humility into the abject, of contentment into the breasts of the downtrodden, and of enduring with a sacred reverence for Property those who have no personal reason to think well of the sharp distinction between Mine and Thine.' That does not seem an unfair description of the total outcome at the beginning of the Gilded Age. The Churches, in the main, provided a means of escape for emotional drives which might otherwise have been directed into the examining of social foundations, and, at the same time, a means of safeguarding men of wealth by limiting their obligation to that sense of stewardship through which the early Church made its peace with the Roman world. (271)

This is, I think, the central dynamic of the function performed by the American Churches when stripped of all but its essentials. They have ceased themselves to make the standards of value for the secular society about them; on the contrary, their own standards of value are given to them by the secular world. They are agents, no doubt powerful agents, in the task of maintaining a social order which is often resented, frequently attacked, and, often enough, so operated as to provoke open challenge from those who are excluded from its benefits. Their real, if half-hidden, function is to repress the critical faculty in their members. They affirm, they dogmatize; they expose a revelation which they insist can be denied only at the peril of salvation. In large degree they seek to divorce reason from experience; and thereby they put the minds of men in a mould or routine of which the result is normally an intellectual passivity before any issue which touches foundations. They create an atmosphere which tends to acquiescence in the habitual; and the outcome of this tendency is a persuasion to identify the habitual with the necessary. (322)

THE EUROPEANIZATION OF AMERICA?

[T]he peculiar complex of qualities we call Americanism is now subject to much the same forces as the peculiar complex we call Europeanism. Those forces will have a retarded effect in their American expression, partly because America is so much more vast and wealthy than Europe, so that it is able to withstand crisis for a longer period; and partly because these forces have to make their way against the resistance of ideas inherited from an earlier America, just as social forces in Europe have to make their way against ideas inherited from an older civilization there. I admit at once, and gladly, that the content of Americanism, in its earlier phase, was more liberal and more democratic than anything in the analogous European heritage. I am not wholly sure that this is an advantage. It enables the proponents of reaction to fight necessary changes with conceptions that once had the power to stir men's minds to resistance in the name of progress; the new purpose conceals itself beneath the old idea. . . .

But it is precisely this false magic which clings to the concepts of Americanism. People still vote for the Republican or the Democratic party in the belief that they stand for separate philosophies and separate interests. That was not, at any rate, Lord Bryce's view. 'Neither party,' he wrote, 'has anything to say on . . . [vital] issues; neither party has any clean-cut principles, any distinctive tenets. Both have traditions. Both claim to have tendencies. Both have certainly war cries, organizations, interests enlisted in their support. But those interests are, in the main, the interests of getting, or keeping, the patronage of the government. Distinctive tenets and policies, points of political doctrine and points of political practice, have all but vanished. They have not been thrown away, but have been stripped away by time and the progress of events, fulfilling some policies, blotting out others. All has been lost except office or the hope of it.' (756)

Selected Writings on Harold Laski and *The American Democracy*

Herbert Andrew Deane, *The Political Ideas of Harold J. Laski.* New York: Columbia University Press, 1954. Does an excellent job in placing Laski's writings in the context of the major themes of modern political thought.

Isaac Kramnick, *Harold Laski: A Life on the Left.* London: Hamish Hamilton, 1993. This may well be the definitive biography of Laski.

Kingsley Martin, *Harold Laski: A Biographical Memoir.* London: Victor Gollanz, 1953. This sympathetic biography includes a chapter on 'Harold Laski and American Democracy'.

Laski's unpublished correspondence with Justice Felix Frankfurter of the United States Supreme Court is kept at Harvard University.

Best known as one of the leading intellectuals of modern feminism, Simone de Beauvoir was an important figure in the post-World War II French left. (*By Roger Wild, c. 1950, provided by Cultural Services of the French Embassy, Washington, DC.*)

Chapter 6

❦

THE AMBIVALENT SOJOURNER:

Simone de Beauvoir,
America Day by Day (1948)

America is one of the pivotal points of the world, where the future of man is being played out. To 'like' America, to 'dislike' it—these words have no meaning. It is a battlefield, and you can only become passionate about the battle it is waging with itself, in which the stakes are beyond measure. (389)

Simone de Beauvoir's name will forever be linked to feminism. Her massive and erudite tome, *Le Deuxième Sexe* (*The Second Sex*), established her as one of the intellectual founders of the modern feminist movement over a decade before the publication of Betty Friedan's *The Female Mystique* and Germaine Greer's *The Female Eunuch*. She is also inseparably linked to French existentialist philosophy and to Jean-Paul Sartre, existentialism's leading thinker and her consort throughout her adult life. Her name evokes Les Deux Magots and the Café Flore, favorite haunts of the left-wing intelligentsia who dominated the postwar intellectual scene in France, and that continue to attract visitors eager to experience something of the intellectual buzz of that remarkable generation.

Simone de Beauvoir (1908–86) is not, it must be said, immediately associated with America in the way that the most famous of French visitors to America, Alexis de Tocqueville, is. *America Day by Day*, Beauvoir's reflections on the four months she spent in the United States in 1947, was translated into English in 1952 but received relatively little attention and was not reprinted by the book's English publisher. English-language reviews of *America Day by Day* tended to be critical and even dismissive. It was not until 1999, when the University of California Press published a new translation of *L'Amérique au jour le jour* that Beauvoir's important analysis of American society and politics became readily accessible to an

All references to *America Day by Day* in this book are from the Carol Cosman translation (Berkeley: University of California Press, 1999).

English-language readership, the first English edition having lapsed into obscurity.

Can a work that languished in obscurity for much of its life, and which is seldom given more than a brief mention in analyses of Beauvoir's oeuvre, really be worthy of inclusion in an elite circle alongside such acknowledged greats as Tocqueville, Bryce, Myrdal, and Laski? Some justification is, I think, required. It is clear that Beauvoir, who spent only four months in the United States before writing *America Day by Day*, and mere days in some of the country's important cities and regions, did not know her subject as well as the other foreigners whose classic interpretations of American politics are examined in the previous chapters. Moreover, one would be hard-pressed to make the argument that her insights and interpretations attain the heights reached by her justly renowned predecessors. In some ways Beauvoir appears to be an intellectual tourist compared to these others. Her empirical observations are shallow when placed alongside those of Bryce or Myrdal, and the theoretical sweep of her gaze is pinched when judged by that of Tocqueville or Laski.

The unique value of Beauvoir's interpretation of America, and what makes her worthy of being grouped with the acknowledged classics, is that it represents a bridge to more recent perspectives on America and its significance in world history. Beauvoir is interested in class, race relations, the struggle between equality and individual freedom, and the other issues that concerned her predecessors. But there is in *America Day by Day* the clear beginning of a postmodern way of interpreting America that would later be developed by such fellow Europeans as Umberto Ecco and Jean Baudrillard. When she observes upon her arrival in New York that 'I've landed not only in a foreign country but in another world—an autonomous, separate world' (13), Beauvoir is saying that the distance between the Old World and the New is not merely a matter of physical distance and culture. The usual continua—more or less egalitarian, more or less individualistic, greater or lesser socio-economic mobility, etc.—do not adequately capture that difference between the Old and New Worlds. There is, she recognizes, a *discontinuity* between the European and American experience that strikes her at the beginning of her visit and that she struggles to understand as she immerses herself in American society, much as an anthropologist might plunge into the lives of a strange tribe she is studying.

Beauvoir's methodology resembles that of participant-observation, pioneered by anthropologists. Early in her journal she writes that 'If I want to decode New York, I must meet New Yorkers' (10), and later, 'Americans must initiate me into America' (30). Her method for acquiring information about and understanding of America is significantly different from those of Tocqueville, Bryce, Myrdal, and Laski. Reading *America Day by Day* one is struck by the countless hours spent at jazz clubs, bars, and parties that routinely went until sunrise. The entire four months of her visit seem to be awash in whisky—with occasional interruptions for beer in Texas and 'zombies' in New Orleans. Although Beauvoir met hundreds of people, she was often in the company of a much smaller set of intimates that included the African-American writer Richard Wright and his wife, James T. Farrell, Lionel Abel, and Nelson Algren. She met Algren in Chicago and became his lover, an amorous relationship that would continue for several years. Throughout her stay in the United States Beauvoir was determined to immerse herself in the American experience, soaking up all that she could in a first-hand manner.

The result is an interpretation of America in many ways more intimate and engagé than the scholarly dispassion of Bryce or the majestical observations of Tocqueville. Her approach is empirical, but not particularly systematic. Indeed, the problem with the participant-observation methodology is precisely the danger of gaining intimacy with one's subject at the expense of some critical distance and the acquisition of a fair picture of the whole. In other words, if one wishes to truly understand a tribe from the inside—quite possibly an impossible goal in any case—then all of the tribe must be taken into account. Although Beauvoir traveled widely across the United States and spoke to many people in many walks of life (and, to her credit, she seems to have done her best to keep the number of obligatory get-togethers with French expatriates living in America to a minimum, quickly realizing that the ideas of her countrymen revealed more about them than about America), it is clear that she spent a disproportionate amount of time in the company of left-wing intellectuals and in visiting what can only be described as the rotten underbelly of America. To have ignored the shame of America's destitute would have been to leave out an important part of the reality of her subject. But between the slums and skid rows, on the one hand, and the natural beauties and urban marvels that so impress Beauvoir, on the other, the vast middle class and its schools, churches, neighborhoods, shops, and dreams are largely lost sight of. They certainly existed in the United States of 1947, but Beauvoir probably found them to be too boring to warrant much attention. Visiting Buffalo, New York, she observed that 'between me and this village of five hundred thousand inhabitants, there's not the slightest tie—we have nothing in common' (91). Main Street, U.S.A. was, for Beauvoir, an aesthetic and intellectual wasteland.

The aesthetic dimension of America is important to understanding Beauvoir's interpretation of America. More than the other foreign observers discussed in the preceding chapters, Beauvoir is sensitive to the aesthetic character of all that she observes in America. The following passage, which describes some of her early impressions of New York, is quite typical of Beauvoir's style and aesthetic eye:

> Rising above the skyscrapers, the sky surges through the straight streets; it's too vast for the city to tame, and it overflows—it's a mountain sky. I walk between the steep cliffs at the bottom of a canyon where no sun penetrates: it's filled with a salt smell. Human history is not inscribed on these carefully calibrated buildings; they are more like prehistoric caves than the houses of Paris or Rome. In Paris, in Rome, history has permeated the bowels of the ground itself; Paris reaches down into the center of the earth. In New York, even the Battery doesn't have such deep roots. Beneath the subways, sewers, and heating pipes, the rock is virgin and inhuman. (9)

Indeed, she often mixes aesthetic and political judgments, as when she judges the poverty and wretchedness of America's poor to be far worse than of their European counterparts. 'In Naples, in Lisbon,' she writes,

> as poor as people are, they still have their animal pleasures: the warmth of the sun, the freshness of an orange, embraces in the darkness of their beds. You often hear them singing and laughing, and they talk with each other. They are poor together; together, they tend their sick, mourn their dead, and honor their saints. Around their afflicted bodies, at least they feel some human warmth. [In America] the poor are cursed with the great curse of loneliness. They have no homes, no families, no friends, no place on earth; they are just refuse, useless flotsam, regarded with indifference. (99–100)

Without wishing to question Beauvoir's rather astute observation on the loneliness of the poor, it is clear that she romanticizes the conditions of Europe's poor at a time when misery was particularly widespread in the aftermath of World War II.

Elsewhere Beauvoir speaks of the 'scent of money that poisons the uptown bars and restaurants' of New York (38) and observes that 'American cities are too big' (139), measuring them against a European standard that she does not always acknowledge. Driving through the southwest of the United States she observes that, 'By traveling in America, I'm not distanced from it. No dream of rootedness challenges the giddy exhileration of the car and wind' (165). Forty years later her countryman Jean Baudrillard would echo this sentiment, saying 'All you need to know about American society can be gleaned from an anthropology of its driving behaviour. That behaviour tells you much more than you could ever learn from its political ideas. Drive ten thousand miles across America and you will know more about the country than all the institutes of sociology and political science put together.'[1]

Beauvoir's love affair with New York, a city that she found captivating—'I didn't think I could love another city as much as Paris' (72)—and where she spent about six weeks of her four-month visit to America, was almost certainly due to the fact that she found the city to be aesthetically and intellectually congenial. And yet it has often been said of New York that, in some ways, it is the least American of American cities. Harlem, the jazz clubs, the low-life of the Bowery, Greenwich Village, the left-wing intelligentsia: all of this was very much to her taste. At the same time Beauvoir was aware that New York was far from being a microcosm of America (but then what place is?). She was told that if she wanted to see the real America she should travel to the Midwest and, above all, visit Chicago. This she did, spending more time in that city than anywhere else, with the exception of New York. But she confesses that her experience of Chicago was quite limited. This was almost certainly due to her intimate relationship with the Chicago writer Nelson Algren, who was her companion during almost all of Beauvoir's time there. She tries to put a plausibly positive spin on the narrowness of her window on Chicago by saying that 'I've preferred to profit from friendships that allowed me to know a single aspect in depth' (380) and 'because I deliberately chose one point of view, I feel an intimacy with this city that I was unable to feel with New York' (381). One wonders, however, whether less time spent in the nightclubs and seamy South Side of Chicago, and perhaps a bit more time in the emerging suburbs like Park Ridge—where Hillary Rodham Clinton was raised—might have given more balance and depth to Beauvoir's perspective on what she had been told was the real America.

To label something banal, ugly, or puritanical is to express a judgment that is both aesthetic and political. Beauvoir's reaction to Houston, a city where she spent barely more than one day, illustrates this blending of political and aesthetic judgments. 'Here no one drinks whisky,' she says, 'instead, they drink beer in large jugs. The walls are covered from floor to ceiling with huge photographs of prize bulls and cows . . . and giant bulls' horns hung almost everywhere. It seems that most of the cafés are decorated in this style. This evening I'll go to sleep with no regrets. I don't think that any of Houston's seductions remain hidden from me' (216). This last sentence drips with sarcasm. Like Buffalo and Rochester, other cities that Beauvoir found to be numbingly stupid and unrelievedly ugly, Houston's architecture, lifestyle, and *moeurs* were repellent to Beauvoir. This is, quite obviously, more than a judgment about beauty. It is also a rejection of the values and preferences of those who live in such a community.

Beauvoir came to America with expectations and ideas about what she would encounter. But unlike her illustrious predecessors, these ideas and expectations—her *imaginaire* of America—were based largely on the images and stories that Hollywood had created and exported to the world. In *America Day by Day* Beauvoir is constantly comparing what she observes and experiences in America to the pictures and preconceptions that she had acquired from the movies. Traveling across the California mountains to the desert of Nevada she writes, 'This is really where those men lived whose legends enchanted my childhood, whose stories set me dreaming' (145). Since Beauvoir the idea of America abroad has been powerfully shaped by the dream machines of Hollywood, the movie studios that have exported images of America and Americans to the rest of the world.

Although the idea of America—America as a new beginning, America as opportunity, America as freedom, America as a new chapter in the history of mankind, etc.—had a long history by the time Beauvoir reached the shores of the New World, the motion picture industry was responsible for both quantitative and qualitative changes in the rest of the Western world's image of America. Quantitatively, far more people than ever before were exposed to images of America and stories of the American experience. The American cowboy, gangster, metropolis, department store, and glamorous materialism became known to millions in Europe through Hollywood films. Qualitatively, these visual images almost certainly cut deeper grooves in foreigners' imagined concept of America than had the stories, literary accounts, and static pictures that had shaped the mental image and expectations of previous generations. Today it is widely acknowledged that America's export of mass culture, an export that began in a major way with film, is one of the chief mechanisms of America's global influence. Some would go so far as to say it is the most insidious and effective tool of American domination, what Ignacio Ramonet calls 'the control of pleasure.'[2] Not through arms or economic might alone, but through the colonization of the imagination would America's global influence be secured. Beauvoir was among the first to understand this about America.

Much of *America Day by Day*, certainly, is devoted to Beauvoir's description of and reflections on landscapes, cityscapes, music, people, the colleges that she visited, and the experience of travel in America—all of which is sociologically important and what one expects from the journal of a sharp-eyed visitor intent on recording her impressions of the land and people she wished to understand. Yet, the book is also very clearly about politics. Beauvoir's political observations may be grouped under three main headings: political culture, class, and race relations.

1. POLITICAL CULTURE

Beauvoir's assessment of Americans' political values and dispositions was a mixture of favorable and unfavorable judgments. Some of these judgments were astute, while others were based on rather flimsy observation, unfounded preconceptions, and what can only be described as a sort of intellectual snobbery that, interestingly, her aristocratic predecessor Tocqueville did not suffer from. Beauvoir got some things very wrong, many of them having to do with the nature of the American political culture.

The thing she got most wrong was the value system of those Americans who were neither at the bottom of the social ladder nor in the intellectual and artistic circles in which she moved during her four months in America. While deeply impressed with the friendliness and openness of Americans—a characteristic she contrasted to the greater mistrust, ungenerosity, and social distance more typical in interactions between strangers in the Old World—she also judged them to be shallow, child-like in their indifference towards and even ignorance of what she considered to be important matters, and puritanical in their values. But even the friendliness of average Americans, she believed, concealed a more disturbing side to American life. '[T]his quality', she argued, 'has its reverse side'. I'm irritated by those imperious invitations to "take life

easy," repeated in words and images throughout the day. On advertise-
ments for Quaker Oats, Coca-Cola, and Lucky Strike, what displays of
white teeth. . . . The constipated girl smiles a loving smile at the lemon
juice that relieves her intestines. In the subway, in the streets, on magazine
pages, these smiles pursue me like an obsession. . . . Optimism is necessary for the country's social peace and economic prosperity' (23).

The optimism, openness and general friendliness of Americans were
traits remarked on by Tocqueville, Bryce, and Laski as well. Unlike
Beauvoir, however, they did not ascribe these characteristics to the needs
of capitalism and the political system that served it. In fairness to
Beauvoir, she is not entirely cynical about the amiability of Americans.
She is grateful to be received with courtesy and respect—and almost
always with a smile—unlike the reception that she would expect to receive
from strangers in France. But she cannot accept this apparent warmth and
good humor at face value. 'I'm not a fool', she says. 'This respect granted
the citizen is completely abstract; that same polite smile that assures David
Brown that he's a unique individual will also gratify John Williams, who
is unique too. Nothing is more universal than this singularity recognized
with such ceremony. One suspects a hoax' (23–4). The phenomenon that
she is describing is familiar enough. It is the abstract warmth of the Wal-
Mart greeter, the car salesman, or the waitress trained to conform to a
cheery script when serving customers.

What redeems Americans' optimism and friendliness, in her eyes, is the
fact that 'the American citizen does not submit passively to the propaganda of the smile: on a foundation of obligatory optimism, it is really he who
freely presents himself as cordial, trusting, and generous' (24). Beauvoir
observes that the warmth and courtesy of those one meets in commercial
transactions in America are self-interested, but never servile, and their
warmth cannot be reduced to a mere formula for profit. But in the end she
concludes that, although the human warmth and openness in social relations are genuine, optimism and friendliness are part of the ideology that
supports the business and political system, real but part illusion. It is,
Beauvoir believes, part of the false consciousness that enables Americans
of all social ranks to believe in their equal dignity and life chances, in a
society where this equality is daily denied and even mocked by the most
glaring and deeply ingrained inequalities.

Beauvoir's tendency to reduce Americans' optimism and warmth to a
sort of democratic residuum that is necessary to grease the gears of a
political economy based on inequality and exploitation is a fairly standard

Marxist interpretation. It is, however, a somewhat distorted and very reductionist understanding of these traits. It is hard to escape the conclusion that she did not take the trouble to probe very deeply into the lives and dreams of average middle-class Americans, precisely those whose lives and values she found so uninteresting. Beauvoir argues that the young in America are 'passive', that they 'do not harbor any bold individual ambitions', and that a spirit of resignation and defeatism prevails in America. Americans, she argues, no longer dream, but merely and meekly accept the world as they find it without ever imagining that they can break out of the existing well-trodden paths that lie before them. Nowhere in *America Day by Day* does one encounter the idea of America as a place where the individual can reinvent himself and dream outside the box (except, Beauvoir argues, among those at the margins and in the lower classes, where personal ambition is still possible). Generally speaking, she argues, America is 'now a fixed, rigid universe where you can occupy only a preestablished place in the social hierarchy' (312). There is more opportunity and possibility for real individual freedom among the educated young in France, she maintains, than among their American counterparts.

There is something wrong with this picture. Part of what is wrong is Beauvoir's utter failure to acknowledge that what she calls the 'fixed, rigid universe' of the American social system may actually be one within which most Americans perceive ample scope for opportunity and the fulfillment of their dreams and ambitions. Like Laski, she maintains that the ideals of socio-economic mobility, class fluidity, and rags-to-riches/log cabin-to-White House have been emptied of whatever historical truth they once contained and now principally serve an ideological function, deluding and pacifying the masses and masking the existence of classes and the reality of class conflict. But unlike Laski, Beauvoir provides almost nothing in the way of serious empirical evidence to support her claims. Even if she conceded some scope for ambition and dreams, Beauvoir's response would be that the ambitions and dreams of most Americans were not worthy of the name. The dreams of a better house or job, college education for one's children, a car and the ambitions harnessed to such dreams struck her as unworthy. '[A]mbition, plans, self-promotion all presuppose a detachment from one's given situation, she argues, 'a return to the original sources of existence that everyone experiences within himself' (312).

Here we come to understand how Beauvoir could conclude that Americans' optimism, while pleasant to experience, was essentially hollow and that their opportunities for real freedom and the attainment of dreams were severely limited. Her ideas about individual freedom and the capacity to dream are ones that the great American libertarian writer, Henry David Thoreau, would have found entirely congenial. Like Thoreau, she dismissed the ambitions and dreams of average people as timid, ready-to-wear plans that society imposes on the mass of men. When she says that in America '[t]he individual is too busy with telephones, refrigerators, and elevators, he is too invested in tools, to look above and beyond' (312), Beauvoir expresses a pitying contempt that is inspired by her existentialist philosophy, but which also echoes Thoreau's convictions that 'The unexamined life is not worth living' and that 'The mass of men lead lives of quiet desperation.'

Tocqueville was perhaps the first to identify the seeming paradox of a society that is simultaneously individualistic and strongly conformist. The conformism and uniformity of life in America strike Beauvoir, too, although she is not convinced that American individualism is much more than an ideological smokescreen that blinds the masses to their exploited and subordinate condition. Strolling down New York's Fifth Avenue, Beauvoir is first impressed by the profusion of goods and the opulence of the presentation. 'And then,' she says, 'one soon perceives that beneath these multicolored paper wrappers, all the chocolates have the same peanut taste, and all the best-sellers tell the same story. So why choose one toothpaste over another? . . . There are a thousand possibilities, but they're all the same. A thousand choices, but all equivalent' (19). The individualism of American life is, in fact, no more real than the Fifth Avenue window displays that tempt passersby with the illusion of fulfilling their dreams. Beneath the façade of individualism and choice lie alienation, boredom, and uniformity.

Tocqueville was struck by what he called the restlessness of Americans. Beauvoir perceives the same phenomenon and links it to what she believes to be the deception of individualism in American life. She interprets the restless desire for more and for the new to a need for escape from the existential emptiness of Americans' lives. On the surface of American life one perceives frenetic activity and an apparently unquenchable thirst for progress and the latest new thing, as expressed for many years in General Electric's ubiquitous slogan that 'Progress is our most important product.' 'But in the end,' Beauvoir argues, 'people are always faced with what they wanted to escape: the arid basis of American life—boredom.' (386).

Beauvoir does not suggest that this existential dilemma is felt less acutely among the populations of other societies where the lives of most people are taken up with getting and spending. But the American case, she suggests, is different in a couple important ways. One is that the ideology of America involves a sort of official denial that individualism may have the soul-destroying consequences that Tocqueville warned of. Thus, Americans who are uneasy with what Beauvoir argues is the false promise of freedom embodied in a hundred brands of toothpaste, and who see in the feverish desire for the new a form of escapism, are not merely asking questions about their own lives, but about their society and what it stands for. Their doubt is not merely a personal matter. In an important way it is un-American.

Second, even the educated classes in America—Beauvoir's circle of intellectual friends in America excluded—buy into a value system that promises individual freedom but really delivers alienation. She argues that the extreme specialization that characterizes intellectual life in America, including academe, serves to conceal connections and provides a way of avoiding the drawing of larger and potentially disturbing conclusions about the society in which this activity is embedded. Visiting a group of archaeologists, ethnographers, and anthropologists in Santa Fe, she asks herself, 'I wonder if the aesthetes of Santa Fe, sometimes look at the smoke rising from Los Alamos [where the first atomic bomb was developed]' (193). Beauvoir is struck time and time again by the general reluctance of American intellectuals to discuss politics. She found the intellectual climate on American campuses to be stifling, characterized more by conformity and apathy than a willingness to question the status quo. She contrasts what she believes to be the political passivity and resignation of American intellectuals to the engagé quality of intellectual life in her native Paris. '[T]he French writer produces eddies and whirlwinds around him,' Beauvoir writes, 'and these results encourage him in an action that may be illusory, whereas the American does not disturb the frozen immutability he finds outside him' (349). She stops short of suggesting which is the more effective course of action.

Beauvoir lays much of the blame for what she argues are the conformity and apathy of Americans when it comes to politics to the stranglehold that the ideology of individualism has in America. Her interpretation of the role of individualism in American life is quite similar to Laski's, but also includes shades of Myrdal's 'American dilemma'. Like Laski, Beauvoir believed that Americans' attachment to individualism was a holdover from previous eras and that its unquestioned place in the culture prevented Americans from understanding how notions of personal responsibility, belief in equal opportunity and unrestricted chances for socio-economic mobility, and mistrust of the state operated as a sort of divide-and-conquer strategy for the capitalist class. Individualism, she argued, was a mystification that prevented people from recognizing the power that they could exert collectively. One of the great paradoxes of American life, Beauvoir believed, was that in the land where the individual was venerated to a greater degree than in any other, he in fact counted for nothing. She explains it this way:

> He is made into an abstract object of worship: by persuading him of his individual value, one stifles the awakening of a collective spirit in him. But reduced to himself in this way, he is robbed of any concrete power. Without collective hope or personal audacity, what can the individual do? Submit or, if by some rare chance this submission is too odious, leave the country. (94)

America Day by Day was written only a year before the publication of Beauvoir's *The Second Sex*, and so it comes as no surprise that she attempts to understand relations between the sexes in America and the circumstances of women there compared to in France. Beauvoir says that she arrived in America with the idea that the American woman was independent and free, compared to her Old World counterpart. This impression, she came to believe, was quite false. The American woman, she observed, appeared to be 'consumed with catching the man and keeping him under her thumb' (331). Women's magazines were little more than how-to manuals on feminine wiles toward these goals and American women seemed unable to be satisfied in their own company, without a male presence to give their status meaning. As a rule, she argues, American women do not particularly like one another, unable as they are to move their relationships from under the shadow of sexual competition. Moreover, they feel too keenly the absence of men, because only in male company or in the assurance of a man in her life does an American woman experience fulfillment. In words that anticipate the arguments of American feminists like Betty Friedan and Gloria Steinem, she writes, 'Woman is much less comfortable in this masculine world, where she has only recently been admitted as an equal. . . . The only way for her to overcome a weighty legacy of weakness and uncertainty would be to stop thinking about it. But then she would have to find absorbing goals outside herself' (332). These goals, however, are beyond the reach of most

American women. And so they live with the thin illusion of their dominance, based on feminine charms and the domestic reign of the matriarch, while their reality is one of dependence and an inability to conceive of their lives and act outside of the limited circle that the culture imposes upon them.

If relations between women are cool and often uneasy in America, those between men and women are generally unfriendly and even hostile, Beauvoir argues. This is due largely to the paradox of Puritanism. The puritanical culture of America requires that eroticism and sexual desire be hidden under layers of repression. Sexual desire and physical passion generate feelings of guilt in such a culture, producing profound uneasiness in relations between men and women, frigidity, and reliance on drink to overcome the paralyzing respect that American men feel for 'good' women—their wives, mothers, and sisters—and the sense that only 'bad' women engage in lusty and frank sex. In addition to the choking Puritan filter through which sexual relations pass, Beauvoir identifies a second factor that poisons the relations between men and women. Raised to believe that she must rule within the circle of home and family, the American woman fears sensuality as a threat to her domestic dominance. Giving herself sexually seems to these women incompatible with their idea of matriarchal dominance. This unconscious reasoning is only possible, however, because the culture associates sexual passion and behavior with low impulses. In puritanical America, Beauvoir argues, sex drives men and women apart, compounding the loneliness and alienation already endemic in American society.

2. CLASS RELATIONS

Whatever equality of social conditions existed in America during Tocqueville's time; whatever class fluidity existed, such that virtually all white Americans could realistically dream of being property-holders, bosses, 'successes' measured by the materialist standards of their community: these were memories rather than realities in Beauvoir's America. During the frontier youth of America's history, she argues, freedom and equality did not come into conflict. The end of free land, greater scarcity in resources, and above all the nature of the modern capitalist economy— in which decisions affecting an increasingly large share of the economy were concentrated in fewer and fewer hands—brought an end to this era. Rugged individualism, Beauvoir argues, was plausible as the ethos of a pioneer society, but a ridiculous deception in contemporary America. The ideas of the 'self-made man' and equality of opportunity had become myths whose survival served the interests of the dominant class. The vast majority of Americans were dupes, victims of a nearly impervious false consciousness that occupied the status of a national credo. 'The American credo', she writes, 'seems to be the expression of a supreme law, at once natural and divine; it's apparently inscribed in eternity, and no one suspects that its earthly manifestation might have been modified' (295).

These are familiar arguments, and Beauvoir certainly was not the first to make them. Like Laski, she rejected the American notion of freedom as the absence of constraint, arguing that this was a purely abstract freedom that did not take into account the reality of class rigidities and different opportunities open to the members of different groups. In regard to their actions and beliefs, Americans are free 'only to the extent that they submit [to the American credo]' (292).

More original is the picture of American classes that Beauvoir paints. She very clearly was fascinated by the sleazy underside of American society, the rough margins inhabited by the destitute, the addicted, the bizarre, and the dangerous. Some of her best prose is devoted to descriptions of those parts of America that are a reproach to the idealized and rather bucolic image of middle-class America. Speaking of New York's Bowery she writes, 'All the houses and shops are the color of gray bread, of unwashed faces.' Her description of the shelters and flophouses of this district is poignant:

> [F]or a few cents, you can rent a mattress or just a corner of floor space swarming with cockroaches. The poorer New York tramps go to the flophouses, where they sleep sitting on benches, their arms leaning on a rope and their heads supported by their folding arms. They sleep until their time runs out; then someone pulls the cord, they fall forward, and the shock wakes them. Those who are even poorer stay on the street. The sick, the old, the failures, those down on their luck—all the outcasts of American life prowl these sidewalks. . . . They have only one goal in life—to drink. (59)

Beauvoir's descriptions of the opulence and ease that she observes in such places as Manhattan, Chicago, Boston, Los Angeles, and San Francisco is not less detailed, but is less sympathetic than her accounts of life at the bottom and the quirky edges of America. But what strikes her above all—

and this has since become a standard feature of foreign depictions of American society—are the contrasts between the rich and the poor, the huge gulf between the ease and affluence of the privileged and the desperation of those whom the American dream has left behind.

The picture that emerges from *America Day by Day* is of a society of vast inequality living with the illusion that the American dream is accessible to all. Beauvoir does not argue that Americans lack compassion toward those whose lives hold nothing but despair. On the contrary, she finds Americans to be far more generous, less avid for money, and genuinely warm and respectful of the dignity of their fellows than are her French compatriots. But in America, she argues, the compassion that individuals would otherwise feel toward the poor and the dispossessed is suffocated by the false belief that freedom of opportunity exists and, therefore, that individuals are authors of their own fate. Such beliefs are daily reinforced by all of the influential social institutions of America, against which dissenters have little hope of success.

Beauvoir pushes this argument a step further, maintaining that Americans' failure to recognize the inequalities and injustices in their midst is partly due to a national unwillingness to accept nuance and ambiguities that would threaten their certainties about the world. Beauvoir argues that Americans are troubled when the line between good and bad becomes murky. 'To accept nuances is to accept ambiguity of judgment, argument, and hesitation,' she says, 'such complex situations force you to think' (67). This, Beauvoir argues, is precisely what most Americans wish to avoid. They prefer to understand the world in black and white terms and 'to believe that Good and Evil are clearly divided categories and that Good is or will be brought about easily' (388). Applying this to what Beauvoir argues is the obvious falsity of the American credo, she writes:

> People—even people of goodwill—refuse to articulate clearly the current conflict between justice and freedom, and the necessity of devising a compromise between these two ideas; they prefer to deny injustice and the lack of freedom. They don't want to admit that the complexity of various factors creates problems that go beyond all virtuous solutions. (388)

What some, including Tocqueville, have characterized as the idealism of Americans, Beauvoir interprets as a sort of adolescent denial of troubling disorder and complexity in the world. She is almost certainly right in her claim that Americans, probably more than other Westerners, have shown a predilection for clear distinction between right and wrong. The whole notion of un-American activities was predicated on the belief that such a distinction between good and evil in politics was both possible and morally necessary. The 'evil empire' characterization of the Soviet Union and its Communist vassal states resonated so powerfully in large measure because it posed the issue of right and wrong in such stark terms. The reason why abortion continues to be so controversial in America, whereas it hardly raises a ripple on the surface of politics in most other advanced democracies, is to some degree due to this tendency to view the world in terms of strict categories of right and wrong (a tendency that is, of course, pronounced among Christian fundamentalists, who are numerous and politically influential in the United States).

But Beauvoir's explanation of why Americans prefer their conceptual universe to be neat, and why they should be more inclined than other national populations to deny troubling social realities, is not very convincing. Like Myrdal, she argues that acknowledgment of gross *in*equalities of opportunity and empty freedom for many would be a reproach to the American creed. But why must the unassailability of the creed be maintained if empirical evidence suggests that it is a false doctrine, or at least flawed? Beauvoir's answer has more to do with psychology and philosophy than politics and history. She argues that Americans' confidence in the American way, the dream, the creed is, in fact quite fragile. They mask this secret fragility with a world view that allows no place for doubt. The sunny optimism of a Ronald Reagan and his evocation of the 'shining city on the hill' and 'it's morning in America' would have been seen by Beauvoir as manifestations of the denial reflex that Americans rely on when the certainties of their national credo are threatened. '[T]he American,' she says, 'is afraid of the dizzying void that the slightest question would carve around and within him' (313).

One of the recurring themes in European interpretations of America, going back at least to Tocqueville, is the idea that Americans are in some way childish and naive in their thinking. Tocqueville and Myrdal characterized this as a form of idealism and sought to provide historical and cultural explanations for it. Beauvoir, on the other hand, pays too little attention to the factors that have contributed to Americans' sense of mission in the world, of being a chosen people, and of constituting what Laski aptly calls the American *civilization*, relying instead on too pat formulas about the impact of Puritanism on American culture and politics and psychological mechanisms for dealing with what she believed to be—

good existentialist and early postmodernist that she was—the inauthenticity of Americans' existence. At times her interpretation drips with condescension. She argues that Americans are like 'big children'. 'Their tragedy', she says, 'is precisely that they are not children, that they have adult responsibilities, an adult existence, but they continue to cling to a ready-made, opaque universe, like that of childhood' (313). Beauvoir was not the first, and was certainly not the last, to contrast what she implicitly saw as the greater maturity and sophistication of Europeans (or at least the French!) to the childishness and naivety of Americans. When a newspaper editor remarked to her that 'Here, we don't pose questions; we resolve them', she hears in this the voice of the child who escapes the troubling complexity of existence through a combination of denial and self-deception. The fact that things seem to work, and work well, in America, and the abundance and accomplishments of the society, give to American pragmatism an appearance of plausibility. But it is false, she argues, because it is fundamentally at odds with the human condition.

3. RACISM IN AMERICA

More than any of the other Europeans whose ideas of America have been examined in the previous chapters, Beauvoir interprets race relations in the United States in terms of sex. Barely suppressed sexual impulses, jealousies, and fears, she believes, are crucial to understanding the often visceral race hatred that she observed in America. America's history of slavery and racial oppression combines with its puritanical culture to create, Beauvoir argues, a particularly deep and intractable form of racism.

Any European intellectual of Beauvoir's generation would have come to America with a keen awareness of the racist history of the United States and the Jim Crow legacy of the Civil War. Tocqueville, who was uncannily prescient about so many things, had predicted that the emancipation of slaves would lead to even greater tensions in race relations if not accompanied by genuine and effective steps to integrate freed African Americans into the majority white society on a basis of equality (see *Democracy in America*, vol. I, ch. 18, 'Situation of the Black Population in the United States, and Dangers with which its Presence Threatens the Whites'). He was, of course, right. The segregation and often vicious racism that emerged after the Civil War, particularly in the South, seemed to make a mockery of the Emancipation Proclamation and the Fourteenth Amendment to the Constitution.

Beauvoir's first-hand introduction to race relations in America began in the jazz clubs of Harlem, accompanied by the African-American poet and novelist Richard Wright. Observing the freedom and uninhibited physicality of young African Americans dancing at the Savoy, she writes:

> What a difference from the strained coldness of white American women. And when you see these men dance, their sensual life unrestrained by an armor of Puritan virtue, you understand how much sexual jealousy can enter into the white Americans' hatred of these quick bodies. . . . Whites stubbornly believe and say that blacks covet white women with the lust of savage beasts. Here again, they're afraid that white women are 'animalistically' attracted to blacks, and the men themselves are fascinated by their own fantasy of sexual prowess. Their envy extends even further. They readily—and bitterly—say, 'Those people are freer and happier than we are.' (38)

Puritanism, sexual jealousy, envy of a capacity for pleasure and freedom: these are the key elements of Beauvoir's interpretation of race relations in America. In New York she visits Harlem, the nightclubs where blacks dance and black musicians play, and African-American churches, but it is not until she visits the South that Beauvoir experiences the depth of race hatred in America. When she arrives in Texas, traveling east from Los Angeles and through the mountains and desert of the American Southwest, she feels that she has crossed a line: 'something fell onto our shoulders that would not lift through the South; it was our own skin that became heavy and stifling, its color making us burn' (203). Here she witnesses first-hand the segregation of Jim Crow and a level of race hatred that she had not observed in the cities of the North. 'From the time we entered Texas', she says while leaving New Orleans, 'everywhere we go there's the smell of hatred in the air—the arrogant hatred of whites, the silent hatred of blacks' (233). Beauvoir remarks on the unconcealed rage of a white woman when a white man permits a black woman to enter a bus ahead of him. In Savannah she decides to go for a walk in the black section of the city, an experiment that she had tried in Harlem. But unlike Harlem, where Beauvoir found that she was ignored and the atmosphere lacked the dangerous edge she had been warned by whites to expect, in Savannah she immediately feels 'hatred and rage in the air'. 'With every step', she says, 'our discomfort grows. As we go by, voices drop, gestures stop, smiles die: all life is suspended in the depths of those angry eyes . . .

An old woman glares at us in disgust and spits twice. . . . At the same moment, a tiny girl runs off crying, "Enemies! Enemies!"' (236).

Aside from the greater emphasis that Beauvoir places on the sexual basis of racism in America, she accepts Myrdal's explanation of race relations. But her insistence on the importance of the sexual dimension involves more than repressed and transformed fears, jealousies, and desires of interracial sex. Beauvoir's interpretation of the place of jazz in American society weaves together strands of race and authenticity. Real jazz, she argues, is a musical form of African-American expression through which the range of human passions and emotions is given spontaneous and authentic expression. White Americans, she says, understand jazz less and less. They distort it, tame it, and empty it of its substance, leaving a formula, a sort of abstraction or embalmed facsimile of the genuine article. At the same time, she argues, jazz is crucial to the life of American intellectuals. It is, Beauvoir says, 'their only diversion in the course of the workday, their only antidote to American conformism and its attendant boredom, their only connection with life' (262). This musical genre nourishes the intellectual life of America, providing one of the few springs of authentic human expression, an island of creative possibility amidst 'the stifling routine and deadly solitude of his days' (262).

It is not surprising that Beauvoir, an existentialist for whom meaning in life could only be found in one's personal encounter with the inescapable solitude of the human condition, would find the spontaneity and unscripted passion of jazz to be to her taste. But her characterization of jazz as almost the only source of creative inspiration for American intellectuals was surely unfair. Beauvoir's view of white America as sexually repressed and creatively constipated by its Puritan past, and of black America as freer and more authentically in touch with the human spirit that society and its institutions suppress, is pushed to the point of caricature.

We are back to the relationship between aesthetics and politics, which is important to an understanding of Beauvoir's interpretation of America. She perceived real beauty in jazz, or at least in well-performed jazz that revealed the soul of the performer and permitted a sort of intimacy of the passions between the musician and the audience. This expression and intimacy affirmed human freedom but also established a profound connectedness between people. Authentic jazz was, she believed, a form of expression that could overcome the solitude and despair of the human condition, which explains why Beauvoir devotes so much time in *America Day by Day* to jazz musicians, nightclubs, and descriptions of her reactions to the music and the surroundings in which it is played. As much as she admires the general warmth and openness of Americans, her moments of most sublime happiness appear to be when she is listening to the music of Louis Armstrong or Bessie Smith. This, more than anything else, is the best that America can offer her, and it is the creation of that society's oppressed minority.

CONCLUSION

More than any of the other writers whose ideas about America have been examined in this book, Beauvoir attempts to understand her subject from the inside, relying on what she observes in its streets, nightclubs, college campuses, and the homes where she received hospitality. She talks to 'experts' as well, and has done at least some of the more conventional homework on her subject—Myrdal's *An American Dilemma* clearly influenced her thinking and she mentions Agee's *Let Us Now Praise Famous Men*, an account of the squalor and wretchedness of cotton pickers' lives that she read while traveling through the South—but her method of acquiring information and impressions is in many ways the most idiosyncratic of all these writers. This has both its good and bad side.

On the good side, Beauvoir's aesthetic sensibility and literary bent combine to produce some marvelous descriptions of the people and places she observes in America. She arrived in the New World with an imagination shaped by American literature from Hawthorne and Thoreau to Steinbeck and Faulkner, and by the silverscreen images of Hollywood. She understands as well as any of the European visitors discussed in the previous chapters that *America is a work of the imagination*. Of course, it is also the world's foremost military power and economic colossus by the time she visited, but she is less interested in these dimensions of the American experience and America's role in the world than in what life, as lived in America, can reveal about the human condition.

Beauvoir was not alone in realizing that one had to get out and see America if one was to have any hope of understanding it. Tocqueville had traveled by canoe in what was then the frontier backwoods of America. Both Bryce and Laski spent years in the United States. Myrdal traveled by car across the South as the first step in his hugely ambitious research enterprise. So Beauvoir's peregrinations by train, car, and bus, from the east coast to the west and back, were not particularly special. But more than the others she made a deliberate effort to see the seamy underside of

America, the ragged edges of the American dream. She began her odyssey with a foundation of images and information acquired largely from literature and Hollywood, but also from the intellectual circles that she was a part of in France. The people she met and the places she visited provided the raw material for the sharper picture of America that she drew in *America Day by Day*.

On a less positive note, it is not clear that Beauvoir saw, or at least understood, middle America. Some of her observations about American life and culture are quite superficial and some are downright wrong. She visits a bowling alley, which she describes as a large air-conditioned hall 'where, with no laughter or discussion, people throw standardized balls onto precisely measured lanes' (69). She sees bowling as a metaphor for the uniformity and regimentation of American life. At another point she observes that 'Americans almost never go anywhere without carefully working out every mile of their itinerary and reserving a room at every stop along the way' (251). Can she be serious? Toward the end of her four-month stay she visits New England, which she describes as 'the heart of real America' (323). The heart of the America of Whitman, Hawthorne, Melville, and Thoreau perhaps, whose America was firmly lodged in her imagination, but the 'real heart' of America by the middle of the twentieth century? At the very least, this was not self-evident.

Beauvoir has no sympathetic feelings toward middle-class America, nor, particularly, toward the working class except as an object of romanticization. Her left-wing world view was reinforced by the intellectual contacts she made while in America, a fact that she acknowledges when she describes them as 'men of the Far Left who want a society without discrimination, class, or boundaries. With only one exception, all were communists between 1930 and 1935, and later they each stopped being communists at different times' (345). She found their company and ideas to be, for the most part, congenial. And she was astute enough to recognize that even those American intellectuals who were most critical of their society and culture believed in the greatness of its ideals and its destiny: 'Their demands and their lucidity are the highest forms of love' (271).

Beauvoir shares this love, but with the ambivalence and reserve of one who is not a member of the family but who, nonetheless, understands why those who are refuse to give up on their dream of America. On her return to Paris she is struck by a sensation of grayness, leading her to observe that 'Over there in the night, a vast continent is sparkling' (390). Like her great countryman, Alexis de Tocqueville, Beauvoir sensed that the future of mankind was being shaped in America, 'a battlefield . . . in which the stakes are beyond measure' (389). And like Tocqueville, she was not convinced that the outcome would be utopia.

POSTSCRIPT

Beauvoir's ambivalence toward America did not last. In her autobiography, *All Said and Done*, she has kinder words for the Maoists in China than for the United States. By the end of her life Beauvoir had come around to the view that America was a sort of capitalist police state at home and a bully abroad. The race riots of the 1960s and the quagmire of America's involvement in Vietnam certainly contributed to her increasingly critical view of the United States, but the roots of her disillusionment were not only political; they were philosophical and aesthetic as well. The charms and raw excitement that she saw in the New World during her 1947 visit faded with time, such that the young Beauvoir who could describe a jazz nightclub in Harlem, a New Mexico desert sunset, or a New England village scene in rapturous terms was replaced by an older Beauvoir for whom America came to represent the antithesis of freedom and the very denial of a new promise for man. The blush was most definitely off the rose of her romance with America.

~

Excerpts from Simone de Beauvoir, *America Day by Day*

HOLLYWOOD: THE NEW OPIATE OF THE MASSES?

I'm struck by how, in this field—as in all others—these bitter complaints are never accompanied by any hope of change. On the contrary, everyone thinks the situation will get even worse. And it seems to me, in fact, that Hollywood isn't suffering only from an economic crisis or from an overly extreme division of labor and other contingencies; its ills are deeper—America no longer knows how to express itself or dares to admit anything. Neither the living, picturesque tragedies of the streets in New York and Chicago nor the true daily dramas of the 160 million people who inhabit this great land are brought to the screen. Movies show a conventional, *papier mâché* America in which only the landscapes and the material details have some reality. From this point of view, *Lost Weekend* (with its images of Third Avenue) and *The Best Years of Our Lives* are almost unique exceptions. Literature hasn't yet been strangled, but the cinema, which is more directly tied to the forces of capitalism, has already learned to hold its tongue. This silence is the silence of death. (172–3)

THE FALL OF JEFFERSON'S 'NEW MAN' IN AMERICA

It would be false to call [Americans'] taste for independence inauthentic—the sense of human dignity is manifest everywhere in numerous and striking ways. The truth is that every day there is an increasingly radical divorce between the ideal and the reality. Jefferson's idealism no longer suits life today, which is why there's such a large gap between theory and practice that one is tempted to say it's 'pure hypocrisy.' This gap does not come from a secret contempt for grand principles, allowing them to be sacrificed shamelessly for more practical concerns, but from the fact that in their obsolete form they no longer apply to modern life: the equality and freedom they permitted have been emptied of their meaning by the demands of the present situation.

Americans have never demanded an *actual* economic equality; they accept that there are different living standards, as long as every citizen has the *possibility* of rising from one level to another through his own efforts. But this is just where the deception begins. In pioneer times, when the land had no boundaries, when its resources hadn't been exploited, and when the economy was truly anarchic, men did not impose limits on one another through the sole fact of their existence. Competition was truly free, and the words 'freedom' and 'equality' were not in conflict; each individual had his chance as long as he wasn't deprived of it by some specific act. Now, the New World is as fixed as the Old, society has lost its mobility, money is kept in a few hands, and the worker's tasks are carefully defined. Opportunities, too, are limited. The individual does not begin with an open future; his place in the machinery defines the course of his whole life. Naturally, a few accidental successes fuel the cherished myth of the 'self-made man,' but this is as deceptive as comparing a lottery ticket to a treasury bond: every ticket can win, but there is only a tiny percentage of winning tickets. Here, the equivocalness of the word 'chance' is exploited, for its precise statistical meaning is very different from the vague import it has for the individual bewitched by dubious promises. At a time when the economy is no longer individualistic, it's a lie to continue regarding every individual as a singular case: he has only the singularity of a number. Without knowing it, he is subject to the law of averages, like that stone Spinoza speaks of which thinks it is rolling voluntarily when in fact it is obeying the principle of inertia. This is what makes a man's 'participation' in the life of the country assume the guise of a lure. In fact, the destiny of the USA is not played out equally in each of its members: there is a class that governs in the belief that it is serving this entity 'America,' yet the average American serves singular and concrete interests that are not his own. This means that freedom has no more concrete reality than equality. Of course, you can always believe you're free if you stay within your designated limits, and the whole cunning of the ruling elite lies in knowing how to restrain its citizens without appearing to do so. But anyone who wanted to surpass these limits would run up against a wall. The middle-class citizen has no grip on the country's economic life and only a feeble influence on its political fate. The abundance of clothes, books, films, newspapers, etc., gives him the illusion of choice, but in fact he is passive. Many things conspire to make him resigned to this passivity. (293–5)

RESIGNATION IN THE LAND OF OPPORTUNITY

Through a lack of participation in society, [American] young people do not harbor any bold individual ambitions—first, because the one hardly ever happens without the other. To dream of making one's way in the world requires that the world be open, unstable, malleable. Americans still speak a great deal about their pioneer ancestors, for whom life was a constant act of creating the world, and they perpetuate the legend that the humblest immigrant can become president of the United States tomorrow. But by now, this time is past. The 'push to the top' that characterized American life, in which generations upon generations among the lower classes raised themselves up a rung in society, is almost complete. It was linked to the existence of open frontiers and an economy favorable to small businesses. Today, immigration has nearly stopped (8.7 percent of Americans were born abroad in 1940 as opposed to 12.5 percent in 1920). There is no uninhabited land left; agriculture is in a period of depression; and industry is so well organized that it takes enormous capital outlays to start any business—there is no opportunity in America for the self-made man anymore. It's now a fixed, rigid universe where you can occupy only a preestablished place in the social hierarchy. In France, the young workers are in almost the same situation. They aren't offered any possibility of choice, but young, middle-class students can preserve the dream of doing something, of becoming someone. The world is open to them and constantly changing; the future is not foreclosed—it offers them individual opportunities. Here in America, personal ambition is still possible among the lower classes: the little New Orleans trumpet player who had such a passionate concern for his destiny was of humble origins. But in the higher spheres, from which the students at the great universities are recruited, an individual doesn't get any chance to invent his own projects.

Of course, in a sense this invention is always possible; in the most limited situation, freedom can be won. But this reconquest demands an inner revolution. And here we come to a second, deeper reason for American inertia: ambition, plans, self-promotion all presuppose a detachment from one's given situation, a return to the original sources of existence that everyone experiences within himself, a questioning similar to that which Descartes practiced in the realm of ideas. But such a shift is especially repugnant to the American conscience. I still think of that journalist who told me, 'Here, we don't pose questions; we resolve them.' Unfortunately, this witticism expresses an important truth. The taste for simple results and the disdain for the process that leads to them arise from the same prejudice. There are two reasons for this, and one is positive: the given world is marvelously rich, with an intoxicating abundance and perfection. Heidegger says that 'the world appears on the horizon of broken machinery,' and here the machinery is not broken. The world, in its all-encompassing and disquieting presence, does not reveal its true character, nor that of the *subject*, which is its correlative. The individual is too busy with telephones, refrigerators, and elevators, he is too invested in tools, to look above and beyond. The other reason is negative: the Puritan tradition and the sense of sin forbid a return to the original nakedness; the American is afraid of the dizzying void that the slightest question would carve around and within him. (311–13)

VOYEURISM ON THE SLEAZY MARGINS OF AMERICA

'We won't go into this bar,' says [Nelson Algren]. 'It's lost all its customers since the pianist was shot down by a bullet from a revolver.' Although the gangster era has passed, it seems that murder is still a rather frequent occurrence: there are settlings of accounts, private quarrels, and petty local quarrels, not to mention assaults. 'In this bar,' Nelson Algren says a little farther on, 'I saw one man attack another with a broken bottle. That's one weapon that frightens even the most courageous men. The other man fell through the front window—you have to be careful not to have a window at your back when you're in a brawl.' He points out the plainclothes policemen watching on the sidewalk; there are also many in uniform. This isn't a very quiet district.

We enter the bar, and it seems that the customers of the murdered pianist have moved on. It's like the one on West Madison: lots of tramps are sleeping with their heads on the tables, and beneath the 'No Dancing' sign, couples are dancing. A pretty young man laughingly caresses a fat dwarf, who is swooning repulsively on his shoulder. In the tumult of laughter, songs, and the shrieks of fat women being tickled, the dice girl, very dignified, reads a book that's spread out before her on the gaming table. She's a plump blonde with fashionably curled hair, who is wearing three strands of heavy pearls around her neck. I look at the title of the book: *The Women of New Orleans*. We sit down at the counter. Signs on the mirrors say 'No Credit' in twenty joking ways. There are bank notes from every country and photographs of naked women: I notice, among others, some of naked young Japanese women—photos that GIs removed from the pockets of Japanese soldiers. The beggars beg, horribly unattractive couples embrace, drunks make speeches and stagger around, and sleepers groan. Poverty has ravaged all the faces, and vermin swarm beneath the clothes. Everywhere on the walls, there are fresh-faced images in drugstore colors of smiling American girls, healthy and cheerful, with well-brushed teeth and stomachs full of Quaker Oats and Coca-Cola. (357–8)

AMBIVALENCE TOWARD AMERICA

This country so often irritates me, and now I'm torn apart to be leaving. In the past few days, several people have asked me, 'Do you like America?' and I've gotten into the habit of answering, 'Half and half,' or 'Fifty-fifty.' This mathematical evaluation doesn't mean much; it only reflects my hesitations. Hardly a day has passed that I haven't been dazzled by America; hardly a day that I haven't been disappointed. I don't know if I could be happy living here; I am sure I'll miss it passionately.

Columbus Circle, Broadway, Times Square. Four months have passed. It's the same crowd, taxis, cars, glimmering lights. The drugstores and the skyscrapers have lost none of their magic. I know why I love them. There's a fascinating mirage that spreads out across this civilization of ease and abundance: the image of an existence that would not wear itself out just staying in place and would make every effort to forge ahead. Eating, moving around, getting dressed, all this is done effortlessly and efficiently— everything can begin after this. I feel such a dizzying attraction for America, where the memory of the pioneers is still recent and palpable, because it seems to be the realm of transcendence; compressed in time, magnificently expanded through space, its history is the creation of a world. This is what moves me about the skyscrapers: they proclaim that man is not a being who stagnates but one who is full of energy, expansion, conquest. And in the extravagant profusion of drugstores, there's a poetry as exciting as in a baroque church: man has caught the raw thing in the trap of his desires; he asserts the power of his imagination over matter. New York and Chicago reflect the existence of this demiurge of imperious dreams, and that's why they are the most human and exalted cities I know. There is no place here for the dreary wisdom of the petit bourgeois in carpet slippers whose only project, as expressed, for example, in the famous sonnet on happiness, 'is to stay at home and gently wait for death.' To devote yourself to such an expectation is already death. In this sense,

Americans are fully alive: they live in the perspective not of death but of life. They are not satisfied with inertia; they judge a man by his acts: in order to be, you must do. The great metal bridges, the buildings, Grand Central Station, Park Avenue, the airports, the roads, and the mines are the affirmation of this faith. (382–3)

EXISTENTIAL ANGST AND ESCAPE IN AMERICA

You have the exhilarating feeling that anything can begin here. But what, in fact, is beginning? What do people do with their time, with the money they earn? Of course, I don't know the ruling class that studies, invents, runs enterprises, struggles, but it constitutes only a small minority. The majority of Americans are like those I've rubbed shoulders with—they're content to let their lives go round in the same circle. They have neither the taste nor the understanding for collective life; nor are they concerned about their individual fates. This is the source of the sadness I've often felt around them; this world that's full of generous promise is crushing them, and its splendor soon seems sterile because there are no men to dominate it. All civilizations offer men an escape into 'the banality of daily life,' but what is unique here is the degree to which this escape is systematically organized. Neither a person's education nor the setting in which he's raised is designed to reveal his inner life to him. He becomes conscious of himself not only as a body of flesh and blood but also as an organism that is protected and extended by an arsenal of mechanical devices. He goes up and down from one floor to the other by elevator; he travels around by subway, speaks on the telephone, writes on a type-writer, sweeps up with a vacuum cleaner. Interposed between food and his stomach are factories that make canned goods, refrigerators, and electric stoves. Between his sexual desires and their satisfaction, there is a whole set of moral precepts and hygienic practices. Society hems him in from childhood. He learns to look outside himself, at others, for a model of behavior; this is the source of what we call 'American conformism.' In fact, individuals are as different and as separate in the New World as in the Old World, but Americans more readily find ways of fleeing their singularity and avoiding the feeling of 'primal abandonment'—or perhaps they don't find an escape, but at least they look for it with more determination here. Like everyone else, they know boredom, dissatisfaction, and doubt, but they try to rationalize their confusion by posing these as their 'problems.' Instead of drawing strength from solitude and trying to overcome it by examining it more thoroughly, they cling stubbornly to the given. They see the source of values and truth in things, not in themselves; their own presence is merely a chance occurrence to which they attach little importance. This is why they are interested in the net result, not in the mental effort that engenders it. . . . Similarly, they think they can isolate the part from the whole, as evidenced by the preference for specialization one finds in technology, the sciences, and culture. In Hegelian terms, one can say that the negation of the subject leads to the triumph of understanding over Spirit—that is, the triumph of abstraction. And that's why in this country, which seems so doggedly turned toward the concrete, the word 'abstraction' has come so often to my lips. The object, erected as an idol, loses its human truth and becomes an abstraction because concrete reality envelops both object and subject. This is the paradox of all the positivisms, of all the pseudorealisms that turn away from man to affirm the thing—they miss the thing itself and attain only concepts. In every area they rush for fear that the result will already be outdated the moment it's achieved. Cut off from the past and the future, the present has no thickness. Nothing is stranger to Americans than the idea of seeing the moment as a recapitulation of time, as a mirror of the eternal, and of anchoring themselves in it in order to grasp timeless truths or values. The contents of the moment seem to them as precarious as the moment itself. Because they don't acknowledge that truths and values are *evolving*, they don't know how to preserve them in the movement that surpasses them; they just deny them. History is a large cemetery here: men, works, and ideas die almost as soon as they are born. And every individual existence has a taste of death: from minute to minute, the present is merely an honorary past. It must constantly be filled with the new to conceal the curse it carries within it. That's why Americans love speed, alcohol, film 'thrillings,' and sensational news. They feverishly demand something more and, again, something more, never able to quell their restlessness. Yet here, as everywhere else, life repeats itself day after day, so people amuse themselves with gadgets, and lacking real projects, they cultivate hobbies. These manias allow them to pretend to take responsibility, by choice, for their daily habits. Sports, movies, and comics all offer distractions. But in the end, people are always faced with what they wanted to escape: the arid basis of American life—boredom. (383–6)

THE END OF THE ROMANCE: BEAUVOIR'S THOUGHTS A QUARTER-CENTURY AFTER *AMERICA DAY BY DAY*

The moment a nationalist or a popular movement seems to threaten its interests, the United States crushes it. Millions upon millions of men are kept in a subhuman condition so that the United States may plunder the wealth of the under-developed countries at its ease. What is so scandalously absurd about it all is that, as economists have proved, the billions of dollars thus extorted by America do nothing to help the well-being of the American people as a whole. A large proportion of them, particularly the blacks, live in poverty and even in extreme poverty. The huge profits are invested in war-industries and the main result of its frenzied exploitation of the planet is that the US government is capable of destroying it.

As for life within the States, the situation of the blacks, which disgusted me the very first time I was ever there, has merely grown more and more unbearable; this has caused an escalation of violence in the Afro-American communities and consequently an escalation in repression, with the Black Panthers being hunted down, imprisoned, murdered. It seems that the police have succeeded in dismantling a great many organizations or in rendering them powerless, among others those white revolutionaries called the Weathermen, who favoured terrorism. Yet most of the Americans I have spoken to feel that the regime is no longer viable: such a climate of violence reigns in the US, unemployment has reached such proportions, and the number of people maintained by the social security organizations is so great, that the economy is about to collapse: insoluable conflicts arise even at the technical level. 'It must necessarily break down because it can't go on,' friends have told me. Perhaps this collapse may set off a revolution on a worldwide scale? I do not know whether I shall live long enough to see it, but it is a comforting outlook. (*All Said and Done*, translated by Patrick O'Brian [London: Weidenfeld and Nicolson, 1974], 420.)

Selected Writings on Simone de Beauvoir and *America Day by Day*

Deirdre Bair, *Simone de Beauvoir: A Biography*. New York: Summit Books, 1990. This long and quite readable biography of Beauvoir devotes a short chapter (ch. 24, 'The Most Exotic Thing') to the visit to America on which *America Day by Day* is based.

Letters to Sartre, translated and edited by Quintin Hoare. London: Radius, 1991. Between 25 January 1947 and 8 May 1947, Beauvoir wrote a total of 23 letters to Sartre from America. Twenty of them are translated in this collection. The letters provide a record of Beauvoir's immediate impressions of America, as opposed to the reflections that made their way into *America Day by Day*, written after her return to France. Another 15 letters that she wrote from America in 1950 and 1951, while visiting Nelson Algren, are also included in this volume.

A Transatlantic Love Affair: Letters to Nelson Algren. New York: New Press, 1998. Through her voluminous correspondence with the Chicago-based writer Nelson Algren over the period 1947–64, Beauvoir reveals her thoughts on American writers, politics, and culture.

Joy Bennett and Gabriella Hochmann, editors, *Simone de Beauvoir: An Annotated Bibliography*. New York: Garland Publishing, 1988. This excellent reference book includes citations for 31 book reviews of *America Day by Day*.

Mary McCarthy, 'Mlle. Gulliver en Amérique', in *Critical Essays on Simone de Beauvoir*, edited by Elaine Marks. Boston: G.K. Hall & Co., 1987. This review of *America Day by Day*, written by the American novelist Mary McCarthy, first appeared in *Der Monat* in 1952. McCarthy thought Beauvoir's interpretation of America to be quite distorted. 'It is all wrong,' she says, 'schematized, rationalized, like a scale model under glass.'

Karen Vintges, *Philosophy as Passion: The Thinking of Simone de Beauvoir*. Bloomington: Indiana University Press, 1996. A good analysis of the commingling of passion and philosophy in Beauvoir's life and work. Unfortunately, it devotes hardly any attention to *America Day by Day*.

◆

Chapter 7

CITY UPON A HILL OR EVENING LAND?

The Americans are not wrong in their idyllic conviction that they are at the centre of the world, the supreme power, the absolute model for everyone. And this conviction is not so much founded on natural resources, technologies, and arms, as on the miraculous premiss of a utopia made reality, of a society which, with a directness we might judge unbearable, is built on the idea that it is the realization of everything the others have dreamt of—justice, plenty, rule of law, wealth, freedom: it knows this, it believes in it, and in the end, the others have come to believe in it too.[1]

When the Puritans arrived in New England they were full of the conviction that they were God's instrument, ordained by Providence to do His will and create what John Winthrop, first governor of the Massachusetts Bay Company, famously called 'a City upon a hill'.[2] When Ronald Reagan called America a 'shining city on the hill' he was tapping a vein that reaches back to Winthrop and the founders of New England—America as a chosen land and Americans as a people marked by Providence for a special mission in the world. America as utopia, as the realization of an idea, is one of the original and most powerful meanings of America. Jean Baudrillard's statement, quoted above, that America's global influence is based principally on 'the miraculous premiss of a utopia made reality', expresses the idea that the true importance of America in world history lies in the realization of the ideals that are associated with Americanism and the American Dream.

But a utopia is not necessarily a place where one would wish to live. It is only the popular misunderstanding of utopia that associates this condition with unalloyed happiness and goodness. Writers on utopia have known better, as readers of Aldous Huxley's *Brave New World* realize. A society built on the bedrock of an ideology may prove to be a nightmare, the end of history rather than an optimistic new chapter. As D.H. Lawrence writes,

Oh, America,
The sun sets in you.
Are you the grave of our day?[3]

Lawrence called America 'The evening land', seeing in America's triumphant ascendance the emergence of something frightening that was a denial of the human soul, a place that gave rise to 'machine-uprisen perfect man'.[4]

America as a 'city upon a hill' and America as an 'evening land' are two sides of the same coin. The coin involves the utopian expectations associated with America, or what I called in Chapter 1 the mythic meaning of America. Most of the millions of people who have left their native countries for America, to live or to visit, have come in search of something far less grand than utopia. But foreign observers of the American scene, including the five discussed in the preceding chapters, have understood that America represented an important new chapter in human history and that its potential for greatness lay not in its economic brawn or military prowess, not in its engineering marvels or its ability to assimilate millions of immigrants from countless nationalities, but in the ideals embodied in its social structures and political institutions.

If there is a common thread that runs through the writings of the five foreign commentators whose thoughts on America have been examined in this book, it is their determination, first, to understand how the reality measures up against the idea of America and, second, to understand the significance of the American experience for world history. They all *chose* America as their subject, even Myrdal, who initially hesitated to take up the Carnegie Corporation's offer to direct its massive study of race relations, but eventually accepted, believing that his work could help solve what was clearly America's most tragic failing. And they all realized that their subject was an essential part of modern history.

The conclusions they drew about America were varied, and each was ambivalent about what he or she saw unfolding in the United States. Tocqueville worried about the corrosive effects of individualism and materialism, and about the tyranny of public opinion. He was probably the first to identify the paradox of crushing conformism in a society that venerated personal freedom. Bryce was perhaps the most taken with and optimistic about America, but he omitted nothing of the endemic corruption that he observed in American parties and elections. Like Tocqueville before him, Bryce was repelled by what he perceived to be the uniformity of life in America. He also regretted the presence in the large eastern cities of 'ignorant masses' of new immigrants from Eastern and Southern Europe, believing them to be easily manipulable by unscrupulous political machines. But in the end he concluded that no society in the history of the world surpassed the United States in the degree of material well-being, intelligence, and happiness experienced by the common man.

Myrdal was much less sanguine. Although he was a great admirer of American ideals and concluded *An American Dilemma* on an optimistic note, expressing the view that social engineering was up to the challenge of eradicating the deeply rooted racism of American life, Myrdal was also profoundly shocked by what he saw as unacceptable inequality in America. Indeed, in a 1980 interview Myrdal claimed that his political consciousness and lifelong dedication to political and social activism dated from his year as a Rockefeller fellow in the United States (1929), when he 'saw all the horrors in America at that time—you know the race questions, slums and all of that.'[5] Myrdal never came to admire what he saw as the reality of American society, preferring the social democratic path of his native Sweden to the individualism and capitalism of the United States.

Like Myrdal, Laski was a committed socialist in politics, but his judgment on America was, in the end, more positive than that of the Swede. Laski's experience of America was broader and his understanding—except on the matter of race, where Myrdal's insights were second to none—was deeper than Myrdal's. There was much in the individualistic American spirit that Laski admired, and unlike many leftist intellectuals of his generation, he acknowledged the greater socio-economic mobility of American society compared to Europe. But the dominance of business values in American life was, he felt, corrosive of real equality and the individualistic ethos of Americans had become, he argued, a sort of outdated mystification that was deliberately encouraged by the powerful in order to prevent the common people from realizing the truth about their society. That truth was, Laski believed, that class conflict existed in America, that class polarization would inevitably increase, and that only the emergence of class-consciousness among American workers and the rise of a labor-based socialist party could ensure that future Americans enjoyed the reality of democracy and not merely its illusory shadow cast from a time before America was urbanized and industrialized. Class would, he believed, eventually become the dominant fault line in American politics.

Beauvoir came to America with stars in her eyes, almost literally. She begins her account of her travels in America with a description of the breathless impression the lights of New York made upon her as her plane approached. But she came to America not to be beguiled by a land whose Hollywood portrayals already occupied an important place in her consciousness, but to observe and understand the reality of America and its meaning for the human story. Much of it she found enthralling and liberating compared to the stuffiness of the Old World, but much she found repugnant. The conformity and uniformity that Tocqueville and Bryce had observed before her, Beauvoir found stifling. She saw nothing to admire in middle-class America with its emerging suburbs, cars, and domestic appliances. The sheer scale of America and the extremes of the American experience—from the destitution she saw among blacks in the South to the opulence of Manhattan—impressed Beauvoir, as they have impressed so many foreign visitors to America. Her interpretation of American idealism as a sort of national psychological defense mechanism, which enabled Americans to deny the troubling inequalities that were rife in their society, complemented Laski's argument that the propaganda machines of the powerful generated an ideological smokescreen that concealed the flawed reality of American democracy from the eyes of the people. In the end, Beauvoir left America feeling deeply divided about what she had observed, but also believing that, for better or for worse, the future of mankind was being shaped in the New World.

THE AMERICAN CENTURY

When Tocqueville visited America the republic was still young, the Civil War had not yet been fought, and the vast territory west of the Mississippi was still frontier land, largely unoccupied by settlers from the eastern states. By the time Laski and Beauvoir wrote about America, the United States had become the world's leading economic and premier military power. Moreover, like the world's great empires before it, America had begun to export its culture—its values, lifestyles, dreams, and self-image—through what were then the new media of film and mass advertising. This has proven, I would argue, to be a more invasive form of cultural imperialism than the language and laws of the Romans, the imposed institutions of the British, or any other conquering culture the world has seen. Indeed, one might make a case that it is a rather new form of cultural conquest, based more on pleasure and seduction than sheer power and the desire of subject peoples to imitate their masters. Since the first Hollywood films were shown abroad, America has exported its imagination, self-image, and dreams in ways accessible to the masses. And the simple fact is that many were and are seduced by what they see and hear. America has become part of the consciousness of peoples throughout the world. They are not all attracted by the ideas they have of America, and the image is not the same in every part of the world. But from Paris to Beijing, America triggers associations in the minds of average people.

The twentieth century has been called 'The American Century'.[6] It was during this time, but most emphatically since World War II, that the United States reached maturity as a world power, fulfilling the prediction that Tocqueville had made for America when the republic was still young and raw. As America's global influence has increased, the attention of the rest of the world has intensified. Greater economic and military involvement throughout the world has been accompanied by closer scrutiny, at home and abroad, of the reasons for and consequences of this involvement. The standards against which the actions of the United States government, the behavior of America's corporations, and the influence of America's cultural juggernaut should be judged are not what they were in Tocqueville's time, nor even when Laski and Beauvoir wrote about America. America has passed through the Cold War, the Vietnam War, the Gulf War, the emergence of a 'culture war' at home, race riots, and in recent years has become the chief target for those opposed to economic globalization. Too much history, good and bad, has happened over the last half-century for us to judge what America means against a yardstick that was appropriate when the republic was just entering into the fullness of its power.

The Russian writer and famous Soviet dissident, Aleksandr Solzhenitsyn, understood that America's role in the world had changed when he gave the 1977 commencement address at Harvard University. Speaking during the Cold War he admonished America, but particularly its liberal elites, for what he believed was their failure of nerve in the fight against evil. World communism, led by the old Soviet Union, was the evil that Solzhenitsyn spoke of. He saw America as having a moral responsibility to stand firm against the values represented by communism, but worried that what he believed to be the enervating decadence of American society might prevent it from fulfilling this responsibility. Solzhenitsyn hoped that America would be up to the challenge of fulfilling its promise as the 'city upon a hill'. He worried, however, that it had become a sort of 'evening land' whose virtues had been submerged under waves of materialism and whose elites had lost their moral compass.

Baudrillard's declaration, quoted at the beginning of this chapter, that Americans are right in their belief that they stand at the center of the world, a model for other peoples, and that to understand America and its global dominance one must view the American experience as a sort of 'utopia made reality', is not the view of most contemporary foreign observers of the American scene. America's foreign critics far outnumber its admirers, particularly among intellectuals. (Majorities are not always right, of course, as Tocqueville and others have warned.) Their judgments on America include disdain and ridicule of its culture, condemnation of its policies, and reactions ranging from distaste to loathing for what are perceived to be its values. Its influence abroad is more often condemned than praised. Many would agree with D.H. Lawrence's characterization of America as an 'evening land', although their reasons for believing so might have less to do with America's impact on the human soul than with other aspects and consequences of the American Century. Few see America as a 'city upon a hill'. And, indeed, Baudrillard's characterization of America as a sort of utopia made reality is not meant to suggest that the zenith of all goodness and virtue has been achieved in the world's remaining superpower. A city upon a hill may be divine, as John Winthrop believed of the New World. Or it may be soul-destroying, as Lawrence feared of America. In either case it is seductive, capturing our attention and beckoning us to draw closer, to experience what it offers. This is a fascination that America continues to have for the rest of the world.

NOTES

CHAPTER 1

1. Ignacio Ramonet, 'United States Goes Global: The Control of Pleasure', *Le Monde diplomatique,* May 2000. Available at: www.monde-diplomatique.fr/en/2000/05.
2. Ibid.
3. These surveys were administered to American Politics courses at Vesalius College in Brussels (January 2000) and Huron University College in London, Ontario (September 1999). My thanks to Professor Jean-Sébastien Rioux of Vesalius College and to the students at both institutions who took the trouble to fill out the questionnaire.
4. Christopher Ricks and William Vance, *The Faber Book of America* (London: Faber and Faber, 1992), xviii.
5. Fred Somkin, *Unquiet Eagle: Memory and Desire in the Idea of American Freedom, 1815–1860* (Ithaca, NY: Cornell University Press, 1967).
6. Grenville Mellen, 'The True Glory of America', in Rufus Griswold, ed., *The Poets and Poetry of America* (New York: J. Miller, 1873), 236.
7. Quoted in B.A. Botkin, ed., *A Treasury of American Folklore* (New York: Crown Publishers, 1944), 176.
8. J. Hector St John de Crèvecoeur, *Letters from an American Farmer,* Letter III, 1782.
9. Max Lerner, *America as a Civilization: Life and Thought in the United States Today* (New York: Simon and Schuster, 1957), xi–xii.
10. 'Welcome to America', *This American Life,* WBEZ Chicago, 19 Mar. 1999: www.thislife.org.

CHAPTER 2

1. See H.G. Wells, *The Future in America: A Search After Realities* (New York: Harper & Brothers, 1906), ch. 10.

2. Gabriel A. Almond and Sidney Verba, *The Civic Culture: Political Attitudes and Democracy in Five Nations* (Princeton, NJ: Princeton University Press, 1963); Robert D. Putnam, *Bowling Alone: The Collapse and Revival of American Community* (New York: Simon & Shuster, 2000).

CHAPTER 3

1. Thomas Jefferson to George Wythe, written from Paris, 13 August 1786, in Merrill D. Peterson, ed., *The Portable Thomas Jefferson* (New York: Viking Press, 1975), 399.
2. Wells's fears about immigrants from Eastern and Southern Europe were great. 'They are', he wrote, 'decent-minded peasant people; orderly, industrious people, rather dirty in their habits, and with a low standard of life. Wherever they accumulate in numbers they present to my eye a social phase far below the level of either England, France, north Italy, or Switzerland. And frankly, I do not find the American nation has . . . any organized means or effectual influences for raising these huge masses of humanity to the requirements of an ideal modern civilization.' H.G. Wells, *The Future in America: A Search After Realities* (New York: Harper & Brothers, 1906), 142–3.

CHAPTER 5

1. This trend toward the growing corporatization of American universities is examined in Eyal Press and Jennifer Washburn, 'The Kept University', *The Atlantic Monthly* 285, 3 (Mar. 2000). Available at: www.theatlantic.com/issues/2000/03/press.htm.
2. Frederick Jackson Turner. *The Frontier in American History* (New York: H. Holt and Company, 1958), 281–2.

CHAPTER 6

1. Jean Baudrillard, *America* (New York: Verso, 1988), 54–5.
2. Ignacio Ramonet, 'The United States Goes Global: The Control of Pleasure', *Le Monde diplomatique*, May 2000. Available at: www.monde-diplomatique.fr/en/2000/05.

CHAPTER 7

1. Jean Baudrillard, *America* (New York: Verso, 1988), 77.
2. John Winthrop, 'A Model of Christian Charity' (written in 1630), in Christopher Ricks and William Vance, eds, *The Faber Book of America* (London: Faber and Faber, 1992), 157.
3. D.H. Lawrence, 'The Evening Land', in Ricks and Vance, eds, *The Faber Book of America*, 417.
4. Ibid., 418.
5. Interview with James Angresano, July 1980, in James Angresano, *The Political Economy of Gunnar Myrdal* (Cheltenham, UK: Edward Elgar, 1997), 149.
6. Although he probably cannot be credited with coining the phrase, this is the title of Harold Evans's book, *The American Century* (New York: Knopf, 1998).

INDEX